P9-DTZ-604

PRAISE FOR *WITH MY EYES WIDE OPEN*

"The hardest thing we think we will ever do as musicians is try and survive in the shark-infested waters that some call the music industry. Then something harder yet beautiful is revealed to you; God blesses you with a child. Next, the worst case scenario reveals itself; you have to fight the satanic sharks, tour the world, *and* raise a child—all at the same time. Mix in some drugs, a divorce, and a few million dollars and you're lucky to get out alive. But what about the child? Brian did something mostly unheard of; he quit his band, quit the drugs, and raised his daughter alone. Sounds like a fairy tale? Well, that's when things really got bad. *With My Eyes Wide Open* is *raw* and *honest*—a must read."

—NIKKI SIXX, MOTLEY CRÜE AND SIXX:A.M.

"I've never met anyone like Brian. *Ever*. He is what I would call the human definition of enigma—a mystery. And that isn't because he wants it that way. The world of heavy metal music has its own image. Sex, drugs, and rock 'n' roll. And Brian, you could say, personifies that very image. But that is just our own misconception. Brian is, to his soul, a kind, approachable, loving person, who realized his love for Jesus and changed his world. After you read his story, your world just might change as well."

—SCOTT HAMILTON, OLYMPIC GOLD MEDALIST FIGURE SKATER

"There are those who never leave home, never see what's beyond the fences. There are also those who leave home as quick as they can, desperate for the changes just out of eyeshot. Then there are the people who need to leave in order to see how much they need their home, and vice versa. Brian is the latter. His road led him away, but it brought him back to where he needed to be. As a fan, I'm glad he's back."

—COREY TAYLOR, AUTHOR AND VOCALIST FOR SLIPKNOT AND STONE SOUR

"There are few people whose honesty—innocent, raw, and beautiful—can match that of my friend Brian Welch. His story told in his new book *With My Eyes Wide Open* is affecting, inspiring, and much-needed."

—ERIC METAXAS, *NEW YORK TIMES* BESTSELLING AUTHOR OF *BONHOEFFER: PASTOR, MARTYR, PROPHET, SPY* AND *MIRACLES: WHAT THEY ARE, WHY THEY HAPPEN, AND HOW THEY CAN CHANGE YOUR LIFE*

"The Lord said that His people would be a peculiar people. Hardcore rock 'n' rollers becoming Christian would certainly fall under that category. The rock 'n' roll lifestyle is one of living on the edge physically, morally, and spiritually. So it is a true miracle when your whole life on every level is turned around. It doesn't mean that you don't rock anymore. It doesn't mean that you don't rebel. Jesus Christ was the biggest rebel that ever lived. We don't walk on the dark side anymore. We walk in the light. So . . . rock on brother Brian!"

—ALICE COOPER, ROCK LEGEND AND PRODIGAL SON

"Brian's story in *With My Eyes Wide Open* blows apart preconceived notions of how God should work, and reveals the radical love Brian found that reaches the unreached. I love this brother, who turned his life over to Christ and has let Him work ever since. I'm especially blessed by his relentless love for his beautiful daughter, Jennea. May we all live for Jesus like Brian!"

—MICHAEL W. SMITH, GRAMMY AWARD–WINNING SINGER

"What a terrific read. Having taken KoRn on their first major US tour back in 1995, I watched Head go from a virtual unknown to a global superstar. Even as a rock star, Brian reveals his human frailties as he shares what happens when rock stardom meets parenthood. His story shows not only his faith and how he overcame obstacles but the ironies that have revealed themselves in his new journey with KoRn."

—DAVID ELLEFSON, BASSIST, MEGADETH

"I read *With My Eyes Wide Open* and laughed out loud, cried so hard, and was ultimately filled with hope. I was awed by the miraculous. I was set on fire to pursue my own purpose. It's incredible how much fire Brian endured and shared in this book. You'd think these kinds of trials would've destroyed his faith and succeeded in stealing his most beloved relationships. But the miraculous glory of how he came through with strength and genuine love is breathtaking and beautiful. You hear people say how they came to faith, but you don't always hear about how they came through hard times afterwards with deeper faith."

—LACEY STURM, AUTHOR AND SINGER (EX-FLYLEAF)

"Brian's story is not only a powerful and important one which needs to be told but one that I relate to in a deep and personal way. Having had a profound salvation experience on a Christmas break from a tour during my time as guitarist with Prince, we share a very similar life experience. I also relate just as much to his decision to rejoin KoRn, and the transcendent reality of the power of reconciliation and being 'in but not of.'"

—Dez Dickerson, original guitarist with Prince

"I'm so stoked for how God is using Brian in this world. He brings a light that shines in the darkest of places. I'm glad to have him as a brother! Plus, the fire he brings on stage with KoRn is infectious! So glad to see him reunited with KoRn and overcome so many obstacles with his beautiful daughter, Jennea, as told in *With My Eyes Wide Open*."

—Jacoby Shaddix, Papa Roach

"I've been a fan of Brian's before he was one of the coolest guitar players in the world. I've admired him in his greatest accomplishments and prayed for him in his darkest days. His music, story, and now his books have made a long-lasting, life-changing impact in my life. His faith and his passion in his new book *With My Eyes Wide Open* is contagious. He is a rock 'n' roll icon, a voice to this generation, a cultural tastemaker, but most important to me, a friend."

—Sonny Sandavol, P.O.D.

"Brian Welch has experienced firsthand that God is the Vineyard Keeper in that 'He removes every branch that doesn't produce fruit and He prunes every branch that produces fruit so it produces more fruit.' Brian has been pruned to fulfill the Great Commission in the world of metal music. *With My Eyes Wide Open* will wake you up and make you realize that God can and will use anyone and anything to fulfill His purpose."

—Josh Turner, multi-award-winning country music singer

"I love Brian! He's such an amazing brother and great friend. Seeing him return to KoRn was so inspiring. How the original band members received him is even more inspiring! When friends and family are rejoined with love leading the way, it's nothing less than beautiful and exciting."

—Arin Ilejay, Avenged Sevenfold

"I'm pretty sure God has a few metal songs in his iPod. Brian lives a life as bold as his music and shares it openly and honestly in his book *With My Eyes Wide Open*. I'm reminded of the radical transforming power of God and the hope of new life when I think of his journey."

—ANDY MINEO, RAPPER

"This powerful story truly shows the fight between light and darkness through perseverance and complete trust in God. *With My Eyes Wide Open* will unveil how Head overcame the impossible and lives to be an example to many, as well as a loving father to his amazing daughter, Jennea. I give this book out to people everywhere knowing it will impact their lives."

—RYAN RIES, RADIO SHOW HOST OF *LIVE WITH RYAN RIES*
AND COFOUNDER OF THE WHOSOEVERS MOVEMENT

"Brian is a man who knows Jesus intimately, and he carries that light with him wherever he goes. One of his passions is his tribe—the KoRn fans. And once Jesus set him free, it's only natural that he wanted to bring that same light to his tribe. He wants them to come with him on this journey with Christ, and he's going for it, one fan at a time."

—DARREN WILSON, DIRECTOR OF *FINGER OF GOD*, *FURIOUS LOVE*,
FATHER OF LIGHTS, *HOLY GHOST*, AND *HOLY GHOST REBORN*

"What I have always loved about my brother Brian Welch is that he's not ashamed of the gospel and hardcore when it comes to sharing his faith with the world and living his life in a sincere way for Christ."

—CHRISTIAN HOSOI, LEGENDARY PROFESSIONAL SKATEBOARDER

"Not many believers could be in the atmosphere that Head is in and function—not being influenced by your surroundings, but influencing them. Jesus did! He is our model. Awesome job, Head!"

—TODD WHITE, EVANGELIST

WITH MY EYES WIDE OPEN

OTHER BOOKS BY
BRIAN "HEAD" WELCH

Save Me from Myself

Stronger

WITH MY
EYES
WIDE
OPEN

MIRACLES AND MISTAKES
ON MY WAY BACK TO KORN

BRIAN "HEAD" WELCH

NELSON
BOOKS

An Imprint of Thomas Nelson

Published in Nashville, Tennessee, by Nelson Books, an imprint of Thomas Nelson. Nelson Books and Thomas Nelson are registered trademarks of HarperCollins Christian Publishing, Inc.

The author is represented by the literary agency of Alive Communications, Inc., 7680 Goddard Street, Suite 200, Colorado Springs, CO 80920, www.alivecommunications.com.

Interior designed by James Phinney.

Thomas Nelson titles may be purchased in bulk for educational, business, fund-raising, or sales promotional use. For information, please e-mail SpecialMarkets@ThomasNelson.com.

Any Internet addresses, phone numbers, or company or product information printed in this book are offered as a resource and are not intended in any way to be or to imply an endorsement by Thomas Nelson, nor does Thomas Nelson vouch for the existence, content, or services of these sites, phone numbers, companies, or products beyond the life of this book.

Unless otherwise noted, Scripture quotations are from the Holy Bible, New International Version®, NIV®. Copyright © 1973, 1978, 1984, 2011 by Biblica, Inc.® Used by permission of Zondervan. All rights reserved worldwide. www.zondervan.com. The "NIV" and "New International Version" are trademarks registered in the United States Patent and Trademark Office by Biblica, Inc.®

Scripture quotations marked AMP are from the Amplified® Bible. Copyright © 1954, 1958, 1962, 1964, 1965, 1987 by The Lockman Foundation. Used by permission. (www.Lockman.org)

Scripture quotations marked NLT are from the *Holy Bible*, New Living Translation. © 1996, 2004, 2007, 2013 by Tyndale House Foundation. Used by permission of Tyndale House Publishers, Inc., Carol Stream, Illinois 60188. All rights reserved.

Library of Congress Cataloging-in-Publication Data

Names: Welch, Brian, 1970-
Title: With my eyes wide open : miracles and mistakes on my way back to KoRn / Brian "Head" Welch.
Description: Nashville, Tennessee : Nelson Books, [2016]
Identifiers: LCCN 2015027270 | ISBN 9780718030605
Subjects: LCSH: Welch, Brian, 1970- | Guitarists--United States--Biography. | Rock musicians--United States--Biography. | Drug abusers--United States--Biography. | Christian converts--United States--Biography. | Korn (Musical group)
Classification: LCC ML419.W42 A3 2016 | DDC 781.66092--dc23 LC record available at http://lccn.loc.gov/2015027270

Printed in the United States of America

16 17 18 19 20 RRD 6 5 4 3 2 1

I want to dedicate this book to my new hero—my daughter, Jennea. Watching you overcome and learn to stand on your own two feet has made me even stronger than I thought I was. I seriously feel like the proudest dad on the planet. And, God, what can I say? The endless discoveries I've made of your limitless beauty in the spiritual realm have left me speechless many times over the last ten years. Thank you. I'm finally living with my eyes wide open.

CONTENTS

Note to Readers . . . .*xv*

Prologue 1

1 · The Suite Life and "the Cult" 5

2 · *High School Musical*, Hannah Montana, and Meltdowns. . . 21

3 · The Kiss of Failure, the Light of Hope 35

4 · Heaven and Hell 59

5 · It's a Dog-Eat-Dog World 77

6 · Chapter 11 101

7 · Just Like Old Times 119

8 · Back Where I Belong. 131

9 · Going Nuclear 151

10 · What Goes Down, Must Come Up 175

Epilogue 199

CONTENTS

A Note from Jennea 205

A Note from Brian. 207

Acknowledgments 211

About the Author 213

NOTE TO READERS

This is a work of nonfiction. The events and experiences detailed herein are all true and have been faithfully rendered as remembered by the author, to the best of his ability. Some names have been changed in order to protect the privacy of individuals involved.

All has been forgiven and forgotten between the author and the individuals mentioned.

PROLOGUE

L et me see your arms."

"No."

"Jennea, I'm serious. Put down the laptop, and let me see your arms." I reached over to grab her right arm, but she quickly pulled away, yanking the bottoms of her sleeves down over her wrists. She shifted to the far side of the mattress on the floor.

"No, Dad. Just leave me alone!" And with that, she turned up the volume on her MacBook, and Blink-182's "Always" filled the uncomfortable silence between us.

Why this? I thought, rubbing my temples. *Why now?*

This wasn't exactly the quality father-daughter time I'd been hoping for this Christmas.

We'd been staying with my parents in Bakersfield for a few days. We always came out to their place for the holidays, and usually Jennea loved it. But this year, something was different.

Actually, everything was different.

For one thing, I had just gotten back together with my band. It

1

had been almost eight years since I'd walked away from KoRn. But now we were back in the studio, writing new songs and getting ready to record a new album, and it was almost as though not a single day had passed. It felt great to be back.

The funny thing is, a big part of the reason I left KoRn back in 2005 was because I wanted to spend more time with Jennea. She had spent the first six years of her life getting passed around like a football to nannies, family, and friends while I traveled all over the world. Between the constant touring, the divorce, and the nonstop partying, rock-and-roll lifestyle, I figured I had introduced enough insanity into Jennea's life. Now that I was rescued and clean, I wanted to make up for lost time and, for once, give her a little stability.

For a while things were great. I had launched a solo career and I was home a lot more. Even when I did go out on tour, Jennea often came with me. But for some reason, right around the time she hit fourteen, things just seemed to get worse and worse.

Maybe it was my fault. I had pulled her out of school after her seventh-grade year and enrolled her in an online homeschooling program so she could go out on the road with me whenever it made sense. It seemed like the right thing to do at the time, but now . . . not so much.

Over the past few months, she'd become more and more withdrawn and depressed. She didn't want to go anywhere or do anything, and we started having epic, almost daily blowouts over everything from getting her homework done and cleaning her room to spending too much time on Facebook.

Facebook.

Don't get me started on Facebook.

Lately, it seemed like all Jennea did was hole up in her room and trash-talk with her old friends from Phoenix on Facebook. I'd never even met all the kids, but man, I hated some of them. Well, maybe not *them*. How much can you hate someone you've never met? But I did hate the influence they were having on Jennea. Social media had become an addiction for her. And believe me, I know a thing or two about addiction. Back in the late '90s, when KoRn was dominating the metal scene, I was the reigning master of addictions. Meth. Pills. Alcohol. Cocaine. You name it, and I was hooked on it.

The thing about addictions is they take over your soul. They turn you into someone else, and they make you do things the un-addicted you wouldn't do in a million years. You lose all control. And, man, do you make some stupid decisions. I could write a book about all the stupid decisions I made back when I was addicted to drugs. In fact, I did.[1]

At any rate, for me it was drugs. For Jennea, it was Facebook.

I stole a quick glance over Jennea's shoulder and caught a glimpse of the telltale blue bar across the top of the screen.

Facebook. *Of course.*

Then I saw the profile photo. It was one of the kids I had specifically told Jennea to stop talking to. My entire body tensed up. It's crazy how much raw fury a scrawny little teenaged kid can incite in a dad. I had a sinking feeling I was gonna lose it.

"Jennea." I tried to stay calm and speak softly. I didn't want to have a huge fight with her in front of my parents—especially at Christmas. They knew things had been rocky between us this year, but I don't think they realized just how bad things had gotten.

"I told you, I don't want you talking to that kid."

"But, Dad . . ."

I quickly cut her off. "Jennea—no. That's it. This whole social media thing—it's over for you. You're cutting this thing off right now. No more Facebook."

Our eyes locked like two opponents squaring off at a UFC fight. But I'd had it. There was no way I was backing down.

---

1   Brian Welch, *Save Me from Myself: How I Found God, Quit KoRn, Kicked Drugs, and Lived to Tell My Story* (New York: HarperOne, 2007).

"You don't get it!" she spat back at me, standing up. "My friends are the only ones who make me feel like I don't want to kill myself!"

Ouch. That stung—deep.

I took a breath and tried to calm myself down, but the truth is, I had no idea how to respond to that. What do you say when your little girl tells you she wants to kill herself? I instinctively took a step toward her, but she backed away. Her fingers were still curled up, holding the edges of her sleeves down over her wrists. I could see the tears welling up in her eyes. I was fighting back tears myself. But I was committed to keeping it together this time.

I steadied myself and took one last deep breath.

"Jennea," I said calmly, "let me see your arms." Jennea just sat there frozen, so I walked around the bed, reached out, grabbed her right arm, and slowly pulled her sleeve back.

My heart sunk, and a wave of nausea washed over me. Jennea's arm was covered with dozens of bloody, horizontal slash marks that ran from her wrist all the way up to her shoulder. Then I pulled back her left sleeve. It was identical. I just stood there, my head swimming. *How could this happen? Where did I go wrong? What happened to my little girl to make her feel this horribly about herself?*

I'd never felt like such a failure in my entire life.

Being a drug addict and hurting myself in the past was one thing, but seeing my daughter in complete agony and hurting herself felt like a whole new level of failure.

Just as I was following God back to KoRn and getting my musical career back on track, I felt like I was losing the very person I originally left my career for.

Somehow I found the strength to hold it together for Jennea's sake and calmly explained that I was going to find her some serious help. Later, though, when I was alone, something occurred to me that frightened me almost as much as the slashes on Jennea's arms.

What if all this is happening because I went back to KoRn?

THE SUITE LIFE
AND "THE CULT"

I've often wondered why there isn't some kind of system in place that decides who can and can't have kids. Think about it. Any moron can have a child. Take me for example. I was an alcoholic meth-head with a train wreck of a marriage who spent more time on the road partying with his band than he did at home playing with his kid. Not exactly what you'd call father-of-the-year material.

Granted, I wasn't a complete idiot. I did help form a successful band, and we did go on to sell almost 40 million albums and win two Grammys. For more than a decade, we were at the top of the music scene. Sold-out concerts. World tours. Award shows. Money. Fame. Professionally speaking, we had it all. Our personal lives, however, were pathetic—especially mine.

But even morons can change. In 2005, after years of living the typical rock-star lifestyle plagued by substance abuse, serious domestic issues, and eventually divorce, I decided to accept an invitation from my friends Eric, Doug, and Sandy to go to church.

I had just moved back to my hometown of Bakersfield, California, to be close to my family. A single dad, I was trying to raise six-year-old Jennea by myself, and I needed help—a lot of help. Thank God my parents were, and still are, *amazing*. They loved Jennea to death and were extremely supportive, but I was still struggling. And I was tired. Tired of being a meth-head. Of living a double life. Tired of fighting with depressing, suicidal thoughts. I had tried willpower and doctors to help me get clean, but I always ended up with less than impressive results. So when Doug said, "Hey, Brian, why don't you come to church with us on Sunday?" I decided to go ahead and give church—and God—a try.

That's when it happened. I had an encounter with Christ that changed my life forever. I didn't see him with my physical eyes—it was much deeper than that. I saw him with the eyes of my heart, and my spirit knew the exact moment he walked into the room and actually touched me. I was suddenly and completely consumed by a love from another dimension as Christ literally came to live inside of me that very moment. I had heard people talk about Christ residing in a person's heart, but this was a reality being powerfully demonstrated in my life right then.

It's pretty impossible to describe heavenly things with earthly language, so just know that what I'm attempting to describe is *way* better than these words.

Earthly language can only symbolize what the beauty of the heavenly reality actually is.

Everything changed for me in that moment.

I felt God's divine love flow through me, and that love infused me with an incredible power. It gave me the power to break free from meth and every other addiction I had, and it gave me the strength to walk away from a wildly successful music career so I could focus all my energy on the one thing that mattered more to me than anything else in the world—raising my daughter.

God, in his infinite mercy, had pushed the reset button on my life, and I was determined to make things right. I was clean. I was eating better. I was exercising. I was going to church and developing my relationship with Christ. I had officially left KoRn (very publicly, I might add), and now I was about to spring the huge surprise on Jennea.

You see, the thing Jennea needed the most in her life at that time was stability. Her mother, Rebekah, had fallen into drugs (along with me) and disappeared out of our lives back when my little girl was just a baby, and all Jennea really knew about me was that I wasn't around very much.

Well, all that was about to change.

One morning, while Jennea was playing with her toys, I crouched down in front of her and said, "Jennea, guess what?"

"What?"

"I'm going to quit work so I can be at home with you full time."

Jennea's eyes lit up, and she broke into a huge smile.

"Really?!" she squealed.

"Yeah. I love you, and I want to take care of you all the time from now on. What do you think?"

"Cool!" she shouted, wrapping her arms around my neck in a hug.

I was on top of the world. The look on her little face was worth more to me than all the gold and platinum albums on earth. I was loving every second of it.

This was it. I was going to create a whole new life for us.

So what did I do? I did what all morons do. I did the complete opposite of what I should have done.

When you've been a rock star for eleven years and are fresh off of a two-year meth addiction, even when God opens your eyes to experience his love, you don't automatically gain the ability to always make good decisions. And let's be honest, I wasn't the best at making good decisions to begin with. Some of my intentions were good, but even then my timing and execution were horrible.

My first idiotic move was yanking Jennea out of the school she had been attending because I wanted her to go to school at our new church, Valley Bible Fellowship. Then a few months later, I pulled her out of that school and hired a friend to be her nanny and homeschool her. Why? So I could eventually go out on tour later that year. That's right. The ink in the magazine articles about me quitting KoRn to become a clean-living, Jesus-following, stay-at-home dad had barely even dried, and already I had yanked my daughter out of two different schools and hired a nanny so I could hit the road again.

Yep . . . I was doin' great.

I'm what you might call an all-or-nothing type of guy. Whatever I do, I do it big—100 percent—even when it completely contradicts something else I've committed to doing 100 percent. Yeah, I know. It doesn't make a lot of sense. Like I said, sound, logical decision making wasn't exactly my strongest trait back then.

After I left KoRn, I became convinced that my new calling was to become a solo artist and change lives through my music. So I started working on new songs and basically ran around like a chicken with its head cut off, making plans to record my solo album and prepare for a big tour. I was running on pure spirit-driven adrenaline. Passion pushed logic and common sense right out the window, and for a few short weeks, I was convinced that by year's end I would start touring full time again—*and* be there for Jennea at the same time. Then one day I woke up and realized I was being an idiot.

I had made a promise to my daughter, and I needed to keep my word. I still felt called to reach out to people through my music, but for now anyway, the world would have to wait. There was one little girl who had already been waiting for me long enough.

So later that summer I let the nanny go, along with the solo-tour plans, and Jennea and I packed up and moved to Phoenix, Arizona. It was a fresh start. Just the two of us. I bought us a beautiful little three-bedroom house right at the base of a rocky, Arizona desert–looking mountain. It was a great neighborhood with nice families and close to a solid school system. Typical suburbia. Very stable and very normal. In fact, the only weird thing in the whole neighborhood was me.

The first time I took Jennea to her new school, I dropped her off in my humongous Hummer. It was all decked out with a crazy paint job, red flames on the sides, and a lift kit that raised it up twelve inches. That thing was a beast.

When I pulled up in the parking lot, the kids all screamed, "Look at that truck! That thing is soooo cool!"

One kid even asked me, "Are you a rock star or something?"

Elementary-school kids are so easy to impress.

Still, we were trying to keep a low profile, so I eventually donated the Hummer to the Dream Center in Los Angeles and got myself a slightly more sensible Ford Magnum. I tinted the windows and the thing had really cool rims, so it was a modest-yet-still-very-cool-looking new ride.

After our flashy entrance that first day, though, I decided it might be a good idea to meet with Jennea's principal and explain our situation. And to my surprise, it turned out that this was by far the coolest principal I'd ever met, which also turned out to be helpful because we quickly ran into a few bumps with some of the other parents.

One day, shortly after meeting the principal, something rather odd yet comical happened after I picked Jennea up from school. It turns out a very troubled mother came into the principal's office to voice a serious concern. Apparently, there was "a strange man in the parking lot with long hair and lots of tattoos." Needless to say, she was extremely worried for the children's safety.

"Was he skinny with long, straight black hair?" the principal asked.

"Yes, exactly!" the woman answered excitedly, thinking she was doing her civic duty by calling out the scary loser in the parking lot.

"Oh, no, that's only Brian Welch, Jennea's dad. He's a sweetheart. Loves Jesus. He's harmless," said the principal with a laugh.

Sadly, I think she had that conversation a lot that semester.

It's funny. In my past life, I fit right in. But as a single dad trying to walk the straight-and-narrow, I stood out like a sore thumb. No matter how hard I tried to fit into life in suburbia, I would never look the part.

If I tried to be discreet and play it cool, I became the weird-child-molester guy. People would give me strange looks, and women would hold their purses a little tighter when I was around. But as soon as they found out I used to be in a huge rock band, I became the hero who left the evil rock-star life because I became a Christian and wanted to be a better dad. But I have to admit, that's a way better label than weird-child-molester guy.

Anyway, as soon as we got Jennea settled into school and the principal had successfully reassured the PTA that I wasn't going to kidnap and eat their children, the next order of business was to get Jennea a pet.

Naturally, she wanted a dog. What kid doesn't? But I just couldn't do it. Think about it. Who was going to have to take care of it all day while Jennea was at school? Exactly. No dog. End of story. So we drove to the nearest pet store to pick up one of the easiest pets in the world to care for—a hamster. I wanted to give the thing a typical hamster name like Whiskers, but Jennea overruled me and named him Cody after the kid on Disney's *The Suite Life of Zack and Cody*.

Since I had vetoed the whole puppy idea, I decided to go above and beyond with this hamster situation. That hamster had a full-on, two-story hamster mansion with a network of plastic tubes to crawl in, multicolored bedding, and every chew toy on the market. It was the tricked-out Hummer of hamster houses. I even got one of those see-through plastic balls that it could roll around the house in. Unfortunately every time that little rat got in that ball, it took a leak. Every. Time. And because the ball had holes in it, the pee leaked out all over the floor. It was disgusting. And this from a guy who used to be the king of all things disgusting!

Urine-soaked floors aside, Jennea and I were adjusting well to life in Phoenix. Jennea was doing great in school and was making some really good friends. And for a guy who had no idea what he was doing, I was doing a pretty good job of being a full-time, stay-at-home dad. After a while, though, I started to get a little antsy. I loved spending time with Jennea, but I also missed making music—which brings me to one of the reasons I decided to settle specifically in Phoenix . . . despite my best intentions.

Back when I was with KoRn, one of our personal security guards had a friend who used to come out to our shows in Arizona and bring our guys weed. He was a charismatic character, and everyone really liked him. After I quit the band, the media exploded. Everyone wanted to hear about the meth-head rocker who was walking away from a multimillion-dollar career to follow Jesus and spend time with his little girl. A few months later, my old weed-dealer friend called to tell me he'd heard about my story and that he was also a Christian.

A Christian weed dealer? Hmmm. That sounds . . . yeah . . . well, he must be done dealing weed, I thought.

Anyway, he told me about a friend of his in Arizona named Edgar, who owned a couple of recording and film studios in Phoenix and Burbank and had a similar conversion story to mine. Because we had so much in common, he insisted that I meet his friend. So I agreed.

It turns out the holy weed dealer was right. Edgar and I *did* have a lot in common. He'd had a rough childhood, and by the time he was in his twenties, he had gotten involved in organized crime on the East Coast. But he had found Jesus a few years before me and supposedly turned his life around. Before long we started hanging out together at his studio in Burbank and going to different churches in the LA/Orange County area together.

For the most part, I really liked Edgar. He was smart, personable, funny, charismatic, and he seemed genuinely interested in helping people figure out their calling in life. And yet the more I got to know him, the more I started to sense that something about him was a little off. It was almost as though he had a couple of different personalities all competing for space inside his head. He'd be a humble man one day and an underhanded businessman the next—though I didn't find that part out until much later. But hey, I had once gone to Israel dressed up like Jesus with a beard and a flowing white robe. And another time I went to hang out with a bunch of cannibalistic headhunters in India, so who was I to judge?

Right about the time I was looking to make a fresh start with Jennea, Edgar and I figured the best option was for me to move down to Phoenix and join him and a few other musicians who were forming a community focused on music. Even though there was something a little off about this dude, I loved the thought of being able to work on my music during the day, while still being home for Jennea in the evenings and on weekends. It was the best of both worlds.

I had started writing songs for my first solo record immediately after I left KoRn, but once I connected with Edgar and his friends down in Phoenix, my writing really amped up.

Figuring out my style of music and lyrics came relatively easy. I knew I wanted to do music that sounded similar to KoRn, but I wanted it to be more spiritual and uplifting in nature. I wanted that same heavy, dirty-edge sound of the guitars, but I also wanted that aggression to go somewhere—for the songs to go to a melodic place that could lift a soul to a reality of peaceful release. As for the lyrics, I just wanted them to be real. Real about my life. My addictions. My pain. My depression. And most of all, real about the freedom in Christ from all those heavy weights that I had carried around with me for so many years.

There were three projects all going on around the same time at Edgar's studio: mine and two others. And Edgar was running point on all of them. There was also an assistant who helped with reception, two engineers named Fernando and Rodrigo, a handful of editors, and a few other artists like me who had followed Edgar to Phoenix. Together, we made up a unique little musical community, and most of us were Christian. The funny thing is, we all used to joke around and say we were like a little cult, with Edgar being our leader. So I still like to refer to our little community as "the cult" for my own amusement.

Edgar did a great job of convincing everyone that he was gonna lead us all into great success with all our different projects. He would meet with different people and excitedly convince them that he felt God was leading him to manage their projects, whether it was music, movies, food stores, or whatever else came across his path. And he really believed he was called to do it. The other musicians and I believed it, too, and from the day we first met, I would have followed Edgar anywhere. In fact, I did.

Case in point: One day some people from Croatia came by one of Edgar's film-editing studios to talk about forming a possible partnership. They had massive movie studios in Croatia that had suffered through some kind of creative or financial drought and were looking for American partners with connections to Hollywood to help breathe life into the entertainment business in their country again. How they stumbled upon Edgar, I have no idea, but once he worked his charm, they were hooked. And so was I. Before any of us knew what happened, Edgar had arranged for the two of us to fly out to Croatia to see their studios and finalize the deal.

On the one hand I was stoked. As part of the deal, Edgar had arranged to use their studios to do my first professional photo shoot since leaving KoRn. That meant we'd be able to send new music and photos to record labels in hopes of inking a deal for my first solo album. It also meant I'd be away from home for about a week.

Enter the guilt.

I didn't like the thought of leaving Jennea alone again—especially so soon after moving. But it was only for a few days. It wasn't like the old days when I would disappear for weeks at a time. Plus, I really wanted to get started on my solo career, and Edgar assured me this was the first step toward fulfilling that destiny.

So that night after dinner I called Jennea into the living room to break the news.

Man, I really should've gotten her that puppy.

"Jennea, come here. I want to tell you something."

"Okay!" Her voice echoed down the hall. Then she ran across the room and did a dramatic somersault onto the couch. "What?"

"Jennea, I have to go on a trip for about a week to take photos for my new album." I held my breath and braced for the worst.

"Okay. Can I go play now?"

Wait. What?

And so, with the whole crazy emotional scene behind us, I found a friend to stay home and watch Jennea, and off I went to Croatia. And it was amazing. Croatia was absolutely beautiful. It was snowing when we arrived, and the forest we drove through to get to the studios was covered in white. It was totally Narnia-like. When we got to the studio, I was completely blown away. In anticipation of my photo shoot, they had pulled out all the stops and put together a massive wardrobe collection for me to choose from. There was room after room full of costumes and accessories from when Croatia's film industry had been booming years earlier. I was trippin'.

The day of the photo shoot, Edgar brought in about twenty Croatian kids and dressed them up in the most tattered clothing we could find. The idea (which was mine) was to show my heart for the hurting youth of the world—the persecuted, rejected youth, kind of like the kids on the cover of KoRn's *Untouchables* album. Like most of the things I would go on to do with Edgar, we meant well, but it didn't turn out very professional. The worst photo that came out of it was one of me standing half naked with all the children surrounding me. Talk about creepy! I don't know what we were thinking.

Fortunately, we did get a few normal photos that we were able to use for my press kit, so it wasn't a complete loss. Except for one thing: the Croatian guys backed out of the partnership deal. Oh, well. Live—take a bunch of creepy photos with impoverished-looking Croatian kids—and learn, I guess. Edgar didn't seem too fazed by it though. He just wrote it off as God closing one door to make way for another. Me? I was just anxious to get back home to Jennea.

And let me tell you, whatever tears and dramatics I missed out on when I left, Jennea made up for in spades after I got back.

I had only been home for about forty-eight hours and was still feeling a little jet-lagged when Jennea came running into my room, crying.

"Dad, Dad, I don't know what happened to Cody! He's gone! He's not in his cage!" she cried.

Definitely not the news I needed to hear.

"Jennea, are you positive? Did you look really good in the cage?" I asked.

"Yes! Maybe I didn't shut the cage door tight enough last night," she blurted out through tears.

The look of heartbreak on a child's face is unbearable. All I could do was give her a big hug and try to comfort her.

"It's gonna be okay. He couldn't have gone very far," I reasoned. "Let's ask God to help us find him."

"Okay. Jesus, please help us find him," she quickly prayed.

We looked and looked for that little rat for what seemed like hours. And I really did believe we would find the stupid thing. How far could it have gone? We only had a one-story house with three bedrooms. But Cody was nowhere to be found.

For the next few days, picking Jennea up after school became an increasingly difficult task. Each day she would jump into the car and ask with an excited, hopeful facial expression, "Hi, Dad. Did you find Cody?!"

And each day I answered with an apologetic, less hopeful, "No, sweetie. I'm sorry. Not yet."

Man. Where could that little rat have gone? You'd think he would have at least left a pee trail or something.

Over the next week or two, I tried to do some fun things with Jennea to help take her mind off Cody. We went to the movies. We went out to eat. I even cooked her favorite meal, fried shrimp tempura from Trader Joe's. Cody may have been missing, but at least we were eating well.

Then one day, while I was making Jennea lunch, I opened the refrigerator and smelled a rotting food odor. I looked and sniffed around, but I couldn't figure out where it was coming from. I wondered if I'd left some food out somewhere and forgotten about it. Or maybe something fell under or behind the refrigerator. I double-checked all the areas inside, outside, and around the refrigerator for days, but I couldn't find anything. And the smell kept getting worse.

And then it hit me.

The odor I'd been smelling wasn't rotten food. It was Cody!

"Why?!" I yelled. I couldn't tell Jennea that she had been breathing in the decomposing flesh of her pet hamster for the past week and a half. No way! This was definitely not a part of the picture-perfect new home life I'd had in mind for us. I had to find the corpse and give it a proper burial before Jennea realized what had happened. I moved everything in the kitchen, trying to find the exact spot the nasty odor was coming from. Everything pointed back to the refrigerator. So I pushed the fridge three feet to the left, and bam! There it was. A little hole at the base of the wall surrounded by telltale hamster poop.

I bent down to sniff out the situation and almost passed out. There was no question. He was in there. Unfortunately, the only way I was going to be able to get to him was to literally tear the wall open. Yeah . . . that wasn't happening.

So I went with plan B. I ended up stuffing air-freshener plug-ins in every single electrical outlet in the kitchen, and then I grabbed a roll of duct tape and sealed up the hole as best I could to stop the smell until Cody finished decomposing. And let me tell you, that little rat took his sweet time. It was almost a month before the odor completely went away. And it took me years to work up the nerve to tell Jennea what had happened. I'm telling you, being a dad is *not* for the faint of heart. Sometimes no matter how hard you try to do the right thing, life turns around and drops a rotting hamster in your lap.

In the meantime, I decided to get Jennea a replacement pet. Only this time, I figured we should get something a little bigger. You know, something that couldn't run away and die in the walls of our house.

Enter Marbles, the guinea pig. Once again, I bought the best cage I could find. This time a triple decker! Sure, there's a chance you could end up a mummified corpse in the wall behind the fridge, but until that day comes, rest assured, if you're a rodent in the Welch household, you are gonna live like a king.

After a few weeks with Marbles, Jennea came to me with a sad face. "What's wrong, Nea?" I asked.

"Dad, Marbles is lonely."

"What do you mean? You always play with him."

"No, I don't. I'm at school all day, and he has nothing to do and no one to play with while I'm gone."

That kid knew how to dial up the guilt.

"Can we get a friend for him?" she asked softly, peeking out at me from behind thick black eyelashes.

Well played. But I wasn't falling for it.

"No, Jennea. Do you realize how much food and litter I would have to buy if we had two of those things? I'm sorry, but there's no way I'm going to get another guinea pig."

Enter the pout.

I still wasn't budging. "And guess who gets stuck cleaning the cage all the time? Me—that's who. I swear, I am not buying another guinea pig just so I can get stuck cleaning up double the amount of rat turds! I'm serious, Jennea. It will never, ever, *ever* happen. Not in a million years, so just stop asking me."

The next day, as we exited the pet store with Squeaky, Jennea's new guinea pig, she was all smiles.

What can I say? I'm a sucker for a sad face.

Meanwhile, back at "the cult," another bizarre business opportunity had come up—this time in Dubai. Apparently, there was a Muslim sheikh looking to get involved with the entertainment industry in America, and somehow, like the Croatians, he had stumbled upon Edgar. I don't know how this guy did it.

Once again, Edgar wanted me to come with him to try and seal the deal. It meant another week away from home, but since the Croatian deal fell through, I figured I should support Edgar since he really wanted me to go with him. Plus, I figured I had just scored some serious street cred with Jennea, having replaced Cody with not one but two guinea pigs.

It was like *Groundhog Day* all over again.

"Hey, Nea, can I talk to you for a minute? I have another trip I have to go on for business."

"Where are you going?"

"To Dubai."

"Is that in Arizona?"

"No, it's another country."

"Oh. Who's gonna watch me?"

"Miss Sarah from your school. It'll be fun. You can stay at her house and play with her girls until I get back."

"Cool!"

Man, this kid was easygoing.

So off Edgar and I went to Dubai, and can I just say *wow*. That place was off the hook! They have got some serious money there, and it shows. They had the biggest, most eccentric buildings I'd ever seen. There was one that looked like a giant sailboat and another that looked like an enormous twisty icicle that was over twenty-seven hundred feet tall. They even had one building that looked like an old medieval castle. It was crazy!

The whole five-day trip turned out to be just that—a trip. The sheikh was kind of a freak. I mean, he was really friendly, and he looked exactly like you'd expect a Muslim sheikh to look—flowing white robes, long dark beard—like something straight off CNN. But I kid you not, the guy scratched himself inappropriately through his robe throughout our entire meeting—while chain-smoking. *Awkward*.

Edgar and I had multiple conversations with him about the possibility of investing in our companies, but like the Croatian deal, it never panned out. In fact, almost none of the deals Edgar tried to make ever panned out. He always had so many deals going on that he couldn't focus on any one thing long enough to make it happen. But he never stopped trying. You had to admire his perseverance. Deal after deal after deal would fall through, yet Edgar always shook it off like it was nothing. "Don't worry, Brian. We'll get the next one," he would tell me.

As much as I wanted to believe him, after a while I started to smell a rat. And I know what a rat smells like—especially a rotten one.

I didn't realize it at the time, but I think I was actually funding all these trips around the world. Back when I first moved to Arizona, I'd put about a million dollars into an account that was supposed to go directly toward my music project. But even with *that*, it seemed like the music always required more money—money that I realized later probably had gone toward trips and other non-music-related stuff. No wonder Edgar was always so free and easy with the cash. *He* probably wasn't paying for anything. *I* was.

I think in Edgar's mind, he was banking on one of his foreign big shots giving us tens of millions of dollars. Unfortunately that never happened.

As previously mentioned, when I first became a Christian, I made a lot of bad decisions. It wouldn't be long before I'd realize just how bad a decision my partnership with Edgar really was.

HIGH SCHOOL MUSICAL,
HANNAH MONTANA,
AND MELTDOWNS

I left KoRn. I didn't leave music.

I've had a hot-and-cold relationship with music almost my entire life. The experience of hearing rhythms, melodies, and lyrics becoming actual songs for the first time is a feeling that's hard to put into words. It's kind of like becoming a parent. Making a baby is all kinds of fun, and when a brand-new life comes into the world, it feels like a miracle. But then reality hits, and you realize how many diapers you have to change, how much sleep you're going to lose, how much food and how many clothes you have to buy. In other words, you realize there's a lot of work involved.

It's similar with music. Creating songs is a lot of fun, and the first time you hear a completed track played back in the studio can feel like a miracle. But eventually, those same songs end up taking you out on the road and away from your family, sometimes for months at a time. It can leave you feeling a little empty.

Nevertheless, even though I'd left KoRn, I had to keep making and playing music because that's what I was born to do.

Shortly after Jennea and I settled into our new life in Arizona, I started writing again. The creative juices were flowing like crazy, and before long I had written a couple dozen songs. So I gave Edgar a call. We quickly got our studio all ready, called in our engineers, Rodrigo and Fernando, and found an editor. I was ready to go.

Or so I thought.

The morning of my first official recording session as a solo artist, I was so excited I could barely sit still. It was a hot morning in Phoenix, and I was making Jennea a quick breakfast. I couldn't wait to drop her off at school so I could get to the studio. Part of the reason I was so excited was that this was going to be the first time I had ever recorded my own lead vocals in a professional studio. I had done some back-up vocals with KoRn, but the lead thing was brand-new to me. All my previous attempts had been done on Apple's computer app GarageBand, so I was beyond stoked to get into a real studio and bring my songs to life.

Jennea, on the other hand, was slightly less enthusiastic.

"Jennea, guess what I'm doing today?" I asked with a smirk as we finished our breakfasts.

"Um, taking me to school?"

"No, goofy! I'm going to record vocals today for my solo album."

"Oh," she replied flatly.

Yeah . . . not quite the blind enthusiasm I'd been hoping for. But then again, she was only seven, so I let it slide. I was excited enough for both of us.

After we finished eating, I grabbed Jennea's backpack, and we were off. As we drove toward the school, I was already feeling like a rock star.

Man, I wish I still had that Hummer.

When I arrived at the studio, I was pleasantly surprised to find that my engineer, Rodrigo, had the place all decked out with candles and low lighting to help get me into the mood to sing. Rodrigo was an amazing guy. He was also the politest man I'd ever met in my life. Every time I walked into a room where Rodrigo was, his hands would be held together respectfully near his waist, and he'd be standing up, smiling, greeting me with his perfect, romantic-sounding Spanish accent.

" 'Ello, Brian. How are you today?" he'd ask with his head slightly tilted to the left. He had the most sincere smile I'd ever seen, kind of like a Spanish waiter at the most expensive restaurant you can imagine. And this guy didn't just ask how I was doing; he *really* wanted to know. He would sit and listen intently to every detail as I told him what was going on in my life.

Of course, Rodrigo was so nice and polite that sometimes we just had to mess with him. Good ol' Edgar had a blast messing with Rodrigo too. He'd fold his hands together, tilt his head slightly, and mimic Rodrigo's accent perfectly. It was hilarious. But Rodrigo always took it well and never strayed from who he was inside.

After briefly chatting with Rodrigo, I stuck the black bean and chicken burrito I'd brought from home in the refrigerator and headed into the studio. Everything was perfect.

Rodrigo's overly polite greeting?

Check.

Candles placed all around the studio?

Check.

Edgar sitting on a couch behind the mixing board waiting to offer advice and encouragement?

Check.

I put the expensive studio headphones on and tested the microphone level.

"Check one, two, three," I said into the mic.

I suddenly realized that when you use expensive studio gear, you can hear every single subtlety in your voice—good and bad. Just checking the microphone, I picked up on a little flaw in my voice— almost like the crack a teenager's voice makes when it's changing. I grabbed one of the water bottles Rodrigo had set out for me and took a quick sip to see if that would help.

"Let's try a take," I said.

Man, there's that crack again. What am I . . . fifteen?

Rodrigo nodded his head, and almost immediately, the music for "Washed by Blood" began playing in my headphones. I could feel my heart pounding in my chest. A minute later, the verse kicked in, and I started my vocals.

That's when it happened.

I sounded like one of the worst singers ever to sing in a professional studio. The song was in the key of A, but I sounded like I was singing in the key of L. It was so bad I had to stop the song at the second chorus. Not only was I singing off-key, but my voice was shaky, I lacked confidence, and the timing of the words was all off.

I panicked. The only thought in my head was *Run—run out of the studio!* Edgar and Rodrigo looked like they didn't know what to say.

"Try it again," I said with a shaky voice. My anxiety level was skyrocketing. I tried to relax.

Just feel the song, Brian. Feel the song.

I definitely wasn't feeling it. This time I only made it to the first chorus. Once again, I sounded like a teenager going through puberty. I was completely mortified. I'll be the first to admit that vocals have never been my strength. And in fairness, I probably didn't sound as bad as I thought. But I had built this moment up so much in my mind that anything short of absolute perfection was going to seem disastrous. Here I was, trying to launch a solo career as a lead singer, and every time I opened my mouth, I sounded like a fourteen-year-old kid squawking to a bad air-guitar riff.

I lost it.

I started throwing things around the room and screaming like a madman. Water bottles, music stands, sheet music—anything I could get my hands on. The last thing I recall seeing is all the letters of an

Apple computer keyboard go flying through the air after I picked it up and smashed it against a table. How I managed not to set the whole place on fire, pitching a fit in the middle of all Rodrigo's candles, I'll never know. All I did know was that I was tanking as a singer, and I had no business being in a professional recording studio. So I left.

As I stormed past the control room, Rodrigo and Edgar tried to calm me down.

"Brian, don't worry about it. You sounded fine. We'll just keep working on it until you're happy," Edgar said, trying to comfort me.

"Yes, Brian, anything I can do to help you feel more comfortable, by all means, I am here for you," Rodrigo politely agreed.

I didn't care. I was done.

"I'm out of here," I said, pushing my way past them.

I acted like a complete monster. I was totally shocked at how much uncontrollable rage possessed me, and I had only one thing on my mind: *run and keep on running*. I was gone within seconds. I got in my car, hit the gas, and tore out of the parking lot, anxious to put as much distance as I could between me and the mess that had just taken place in Edgar's studio.

Barreling down the highway, the anger and self-loathing still raging in my chest, I looked up to the sky and started growling my frustration at God.

I can't believe this! Why am I even trying? I can't even sing! And what on earth is happening to me?! I'm still so full of rage! I have no control over myself when I get like this! Why am I like this? Why won't you change me?

Still new in my faith, I expected to be transformed quickly—to go from angry, out-of-control Brian to calm, peaceful, together Brian overnight. But that's usually not the way it works. The cold, hard truth was I still had a long way to go.

By the time I picked Jennea up from school, I was still upset, but I had calmed down a lot. I was still really struggling with anger and depression, and in keeping with my all-or-nothing personality, I always seemed to be either 100 percent happy or 100 percent unhappy with nothing in between. I hated it when Jennea had to witness one of my angry outbursts, especially since I thought they were supposed to be behind me now.

Music always has been and always will be a huge part of my life, but in the grand scheme of things, Jennea is far more important. So even though I was struggling in the studio, for Jennea's sake I knew I couldn't let that one episode ruin everything else in my life—correction, *our* lives.

A few days later I spoke to Edgar, and he had a really good suggestion.

"Bro, don't worry about the vocals right now," he reassured me. "Let's just get you in to record some guitar on some of your other songs, and we'll come back to the vocals later."

I loved that idea. We didn't even set a date to get back to the vocals, and that was fine by me.

Besides, I had other things to focus on.

After my meltdown, I decided to direct my attention to making our house a little more like a real home—an endeavor I could actually control. So I hired a company to landscape the front and back yards for us. Most of our property consisted of undeveloped dirt, and since we'd been there for almost a year, I figured it was time. Most of my money was tied up in the Edgar account, though, so I decided to take out a second mortgage to pay for the project. It probably wasn't the best idea, but given my current cash-flow issues, there really wasn't any other way. Besides, I figured it would increase the value of the house.

Initially, I wanted to build a huge cement wall around the front of the house for privacy, but after submitting the plans to the city, they informed me they wouldn't allow a large wall to be built so close to the sidewalks. So instead I ended up building a little three-foot wall near the sidewalk and a six-foot wall on the inside of the little wall, closer to the front door. I also installed a three-foot electric gate. To be honest, the whole thing looked kind of silly. The wall and gate were just too tiny. They weren't going to keep anyone out. If anyone really wanted to get in, all they had to do was step over the wall. But the six-foot wall made the front of our house look kind of like a castle, so at least that was cool.

The backyard posed its own set of problems. The space was huge. Even with the second mortgage, I couldn't afford to put in a full-size pool and landscape the entire thing with trees and plants and shrubs. It would've cost a fortune. So, like the mini-wall and gate out front, I compromised. We covered most of the area with rocks and then put in a small inground pool, an aboveground Jacuzzi, and a little rocky waterfall in between where the Jacuzzi and pool connected. When all was said and done, it looked like a huge football field covered with rocks and an itsy-bitsy pool and spa with a tiny waterfall in one corner. Fail in the front yard and fail in the back. I was batting a thousand that summer.

Jennea, on the other hand, loved the backyard. She didn't care what it looked like. She just wanted to play in the pool and sit in the Jacuzzi, so she was perfectly content with what we had. We could take a lesson from our kids sometimes.

In fact, later that same summer Jennea taught me an even bigger lesson. Shortly after the landscaping fiasco, I received an e-mail from my friend Greg. It turns out Greg was connected to a guy in Hollywood named Chris Warren who had a son in the *High School Musical* movies. He had scored some extra tickets from Chris to the premiere of *High School Musical 2*, and he wanted to know if Jennea

WITH MY EYES WIDE OPEN

and I would be interested in coming along with him and his niece, Isabel.

And what do you think my eight-year-old daughter forced me to watch on TV every single day? Yep. You guessed it.

I started to see a father-of-the-year award in my near future. I couldn't wait to pick up Jennea from school. Going to the premiere of *High School Musical 2* for Jennea would be like me getting to meet Jesus face-to-face.

I pulled up to her school and did my usual fifteen-minute wait for the bell to ring. I had always hated that fifteen-minute wait, but that day it seemed like an eternity. As soon as the bell rang, I saw Jennea waddling around the corner, barely able to carry her oversized backpack. One of the teachers assigned for student pickups that day opened the door and helped her into our car, and as we drove away, I smirked at Jennea like Lloyd from the movie *Dumb and Dumber* through the rearview mirror.

"What?" Jennea asked.

"Aren't you gonna say hi?" I asked back.

"Hi, Dad. Why are you staring at me like that?" she asked.

"Who's the best dad on the entire earth?"

Jennea slowly started to grin, sensing that some kind of Christmas-morning surprise was coming.

"You are?" she questioned, wondering if that was the correct answer.

"Guess where we're going?" I asked.

"Where?"

"The *High School Musical 2* premiere at Disneyland!"

"What?! Really?! Ahhhhh!" She screamed so loud I thought the windows would shatter. "When? How?"

I told her the whole story, and as we drove home, making plans for the big day, I felt like the coolest dad who had ever breathed. It had been a while since I'd felt that way. When you walk away from one of the most successful metal bands in the music industry, most of

28

the perks and invites to concerts and movie premieres disappear right along with you. I had chosen to leave for a good reason, but it was still sort of like leaving a gang—you lose a lot of power and respect. That's what made the *High School Musical 2* premiere such a big deal. I considered it a real blessing, and I was very thankful—especially to God. I knew he was the one behind the scenes who made that special surprise possible for Jennea.

Our original plan was to go low-key, but then Edgar found out about it and called us into his office.

"You guys are going first class in a limo to the premiere," he insisted. "And Brian, you need to do the red carpet. It'll be great for press."

"Man, come on. I don't want to do the red carpet," I said.

"Seriously, you need to do it," Edgar countered. "You've been away for a while. It'll be good for you, for your music, and for all of us. Plus, it'll be exciting for Jennea."

He had me at Jennea. This night wasn't supposed to be about me or my career, but Jennea really would love to ride in a limo and walk the red carpet alongside all her favorite stars. It would be a great memory for her.

Sold.

When Jennea, Greg, Isabel, and I arrived at the Disney Hotel in Anaheim, we quickly checked in and wandered around the hotel for a bit since there was still time before we needed to get ready for the premiere. Outside the hotel we noticed a big crowd of people off to the right where some teeny-bop artists connected with the *High School Musical 2* premiere were performing, so we headed over that way. As Greg and I tried to get the girls up close so they could get a good look, a guy holding a big microphone called us over.

"Would you girls like to be on Radio Disney?" he asked.

Oh man, I thought. *Jennea loves Radio Disney. They must be here covering the movie premiere.* Jennea made me listen to Radio Disney every day in the car.

The girls both looked at each other and started giggling. "Okay!"

"Welcome back to Radio Disney," the guy started. "We have two lovely young ladies with us here today for the premiere of *High School Musical 2*. Let me ask you, girls, what is it like being here live for the premiere?"

And with that, he stuck the microphone down in front of the girls' now very flustered-looking faces.

"Um, it's . . . um . . . um, it's . . ." Jennea froze, unable to finish her sentence.

"It's so cool," Isabel quickly blurted out, and both girls giggled uncontrollably.

They talked and squealed about their big interview for the next two hours. Even though there were so many other kids standing around, that guy had chosen them. And let me tell you, when you're eight years old, it just doesn't get any cooler than that.

By the way, speaking of cool . . . I had found the snazziest suit I'd ever seen for that premiere. It was all black, and it came with a sport coat that had these silver shiny things going down the collar— hence the "snazziest" description. Let's put it this way. When my producer Jasen saw me wearing that suit a few years later, he nick-named me Gator because he said Gator seemed like the name of a slickly dressed mob dude.

And, oh man, did the girls look beautiful. Jennea had on a stun-ning all-black outfit with pants and a shirt that looked like it cost a lot more than it actually did, and Isabel wore a beautiful red dress. I didn't allow Jennea to wear makeup back then, but the girls still looked about five years older than they were in their fancy duds.

As we were getting ready to leave for the premiere, we spotted a few actors from Jennea's favorite Disney Channel and Nickelodeon shows standing outside our hotel. I couldn't remember their names, but believe me, when you watch as much Nickelodeon as we did at our house, you recognize the faces.

"Oh my gosh!" the girls said, almost screaming. This was the closest they'd ever been to actual celebrities (yeah . . . I don't count), and they were trying their hardest not to lose it.

I was so excited for Jennea that I started praying that the girls could meet the entire *High School Musical 2* cast.

God, if there's any way you could send your angels to help arrange it so Jennea and Isabel can meet Zac Efron, Vanessa Hudgens, and the other one . . . you know . . . the blonde, that would be so awesome. Thanks for making this all possible. I love seeing my little girl so excited.

When the limo finally arrived, I started to feel a little nervous. I hadn't walked a red carpet in a long time, and I knew there would be a lot of cameras there. I figured the press would start asking me questions as soon as I stepped out of the limo.

As we pulled up, hundreds of little girls pointed in our direction and talked frantically to one another. We were the first ones to arrive, so they were probably trying to figure out who was in our limo. *This is so awkward*, I thought. Then, as I opened the door, a peculiar thing happened.

Crickets.

Every single tweeny-bopper there was like, "Who's that guy? Who are those people?"

Dude.

I have to admit, I froze a little. Then Greg grabbed the girls, and we all started walking toward the press. *Okay, here we go.* As we walked up, I smiled at the media people and waited for them to start snapping pictures or asking questions about KoRn and what I'd been up to lately, but they just looked at me, their cameras at their sides.

That's when it hit me.

They have no idea who I am.

I felt like an idiot. Edgar had told me I was going to do press on the red carpet, so here I was all ready and waiting, and they didn't ask me one thing. I started to wonder if Edgar had even told anyone I was going to be there. At red carpet events, the press is informed about the names and titles of everyone walking—that is, unless Edgar is in charge of letting them know.

After a couple of awkward seconds just standing there waiting for questions that never came, we grabbed the girls and headed toward the theater. I was a little irritated, but I quickly reminded myself that tonight wasn't about me. I shook it off and followed a still extremely excited Jennea into the lobby.

It was definitely a star-studded evening. David Beckham and his wife, Victoria, were there with their kids. Vanessa Williams was there with her kids too. And it looked like every star from the Disney Channel and Nickelodeon was there—except for Miley Cyrus, one of Jennea's favorites.

After sitting through what was quite possibly the worst movie I'd ever seen in my entire life, the lights came on, and we stayed seated so the girls could scope out all the stars getting ready to exit. That's when we heard the voice.

"Y'all 'bout ready to get outta here?"

We quickly turned around, and when we saw who it was, Jennea and her friend about died.

It was Billy Ray Cyrus, and right next to him was Hannah Montana herself.

"Well, how you girls doin' tonight?" Billy asked the girls. "Y'all wanna say hi to Miley?"

Unbelievable. They had been sitting directly behind us all night, and we didn't even realize it.

"Hi!" Miley chirped, smiling.

The girls were completely starstruck. "Um . . . hi," they stammered, their faces bright red. I wish I could've gotten a picture of that moment. Unfortunately, everyone was rushing to get going, so I wasn't able to snap a photo of Miley with the girls.

Still, I was hoping my earlier request to God about meeting the rest of the cast would come through at the after-party we were invited to attend. They were definitely going to be there, but meeting them wasn't going to be easy.

While the movie theater was small and only fit a certain number of people, the after-party was slammed with hundreds of kids, all swarming like crazy around the young celebrities. We tried to make our way through the crowd, but it was just too crazy. We ended up meeting a couple of actors from *Hannah Montana* and some other shows Jennea liked, but most of the *High School Musical 2* cast took off early.

As the party started winding down and the actors began clocking out, we headed back toward the hotel to go to our rooms and collapse. I was disappointed that the girls didn't get to meet the stars of the movie, but just when I thought the night was over, our host for the night, Chris Warren, came to save the day again. He walked up to me and asked, "Hey, do the girls want to meet the cast? Most of them are in Zac Efron's hotel room."

God had come through at the last second, bases loaded at the bottom of the ninth. This was *way* better than getting Jennea a puppy. And as an added bonus, I didn't have to clean up after anything!

That night we met all the actors in the movie: Lucas Grabeel, Monique Coleman, Ashley Tisdale (aka the blonde I couldn't remember), KayCee Stroh, and Chris Warren Jr. But when Zac Efron and Vanessa Hudgens came out, I saw a blushing expression on Jennea's face I'd never seen in her eight short years of life. She was floored.

Since the girls couldn't utter a single word, I introduced myself first.

"Hey, my name's Brian. Nice to meet you," I said, reaching out to shake Zac's hand. "You guys are on my TV screen every single day, so I feel like I know you already."

"Haha, same with you," Zac said, smiling. "I used to see you guys on MTV every day."

After we talked for a few minutes, I took some photos of Jennea and Isabel with Zac and Vanessa, then we all headed upstairs to our rooms. It was the perfect ending to a perfect night that my little girl would remember forever.

I may not have been a crowd-stopping rock star, but I was racking up some pretty big points as a dad, and in my book, that was far more important.

But sometimes good things must come to an end. While I was off hobnobbing with teen stars in Los Angeles, Edgar had been hard at work at "the cult," making promises, cutting deals, and spending money. And, as it turned out, my name was attached to almost all of it. On top of that, the pressure from Edgar mixed with my own personal failures and music career disappointments would soon drag me down into such a dark depression that I seriously didn't know how I would get out.

Things were about to get ugly.

THE KISS OF FAILURE, THE LIGHT OF HOPE

Brian, have a seat, please," Rodrigo began. "We want to tell you about a small problem we are having."

I sat down and tried to get a read on Edgar's and Rodrigo's faces. It had been a couple of months since my epic studio meltdown, and at Edgar's suggestion, we had been focusing primarily on laying down some musical tracks to keep things moving forward while I got my head back on straight. Though for the life of me, I couldn't figure out what the problem was.

We had just finished recording Josh Freese's drum tracks, and they were incredible. But then, why wouldn't they be? Josh had also done tracks for Nine Inch Nails, Katy Perry, Kelly Clarkson, and Guns N' Roses. The guy was a pro.

"We didn't seem to get a very good recording of Josh's drums," Rodrigo continued. "How would you feel about Steve Gadd recording some of the songs over?"

"What do you mean? Josh killed it on those tracks!" I shot back.

"I know, bro," Edgar cut in. "But the sound quality just isn't what we thought it was. We think the low ceiling in the studio may be the reason the drum tones are sounding flat and stale. Besides, Steve Gadd is a legend. He's been around forever, and he'd be a great fit for your live band when you start touring. I think we should give it a try."

I couldn't think of a counterargument. Not only was Edgar an extremely convincing guy, but in this case, he was also right—Steve Gadd was a legend. As much as I loved Josh's tracks, I agreed to give Steve a shot. And I have to admit, the guy sounded good.

Not only was Steve a legendary drummer, he was also a great guy, and over the next few months we all spent some time hanging out with him and his wife. They were incredible people, and everything was going great, until . . .

It turned out Edgar had promised Steve all kinds of work and had encouraged him and his wife to move to Arizona. The problem was, there wasn't any money coming in. Edgar couldn't even pay Steve for the tracks we'd already recorded. Needless to say, Steve and his wife got pretty ticked off, and I couldn't blame them. After all, Steve had been in the music business a long time. It's bad enough pulling something like this on a rookie, but to pull it on a pro like Steve Gadd? That's just beyond messed up.

Once Steve realized he wasn't getting paid, he and his wife blew up at Edgar one afternoon at the studio and took off. The rest of us stuck by Edgar out of loyalty, but seeing all that go down and hearing Steve lay into Edgar about all the false promises he'd made definitely concerned us all. Edgar always had a great excuse though. Somehow he'd always manage to blame it on the other person.

"Don't worry about Steve," Edgar reassured us. "He's got some ego and entitlement issues he needs to go work on." And just in case we still weren't convinced, Edgar shifted his focus to inflating *our* egos: "He just doesn't know how to walk by faith and trust in God like us."

Looking back, it's easy to see that the wheels were starting to come off the bus, but as a new, naïve Christian, I bought into his spin on faith. I chose to ignore the glaring warning signs. Every time something bad happened, I took it as a challenge to see if I could, in fact, put all my trust in God. But I'd eventually come to realize that trusting God and trusting Edgar were two entirely different things.

By this point I had been connected to Edgar for a little over a year and a half, and in that time he had made dozens of promises to me and to others in "the cult," but nothing ever came of them. It seemed like whenever we took one step forward, we took three steps back.

For example, we'd been talking to a few big-name record labels about partnering with them so they could help us start our own smaller, independent label to release not only my first solo album, but the albums of all the other musicians Edgar made promises to as well. The plan was to distribute all our record label's releases through a big-name label's distribution umbrella. But every time the talks got close to completion, an executive of one of the labels would either get sick, have a family member fall deathly ill, or they'd resign from their department and disappear completely. And each time, Edgar would wave it off as a sign that they weren't the right label.

Still, each time a label would back out, it was a crushing disappointment. I tried with all my might to remain at peace and take an easygoing attitude, but it was really difficult balancing my faith with what was starting to seem like constant disappointment.

After the first two or three labels backed out, we came super close to finalizing a deal with a company called Ryko Distribution. Everyone who had been involved made it sound as though it was practically a done deal. I was stoked. I still hadn't set a date to finish recording my vocals because without a label there didn't seem to be any urgency. Once we inked a deal, though, that was going to be my cue to get back in there and make it happen. But once again, the deal fell through. I have no idea why. Maybe it was because the Ryko guys were leery of Edgar. Or maybe the whole faith thing scared them off.

I don't know. All I remember is how much burning anger I felt beginning to simmer inside again.

"Why does this keep happening?" I half asked, half accused Edgar. "We keep wasting our time talking to these idiots for months and then nothing! Why?"

Then Edgar did what Edgar did best. He played the God card. "Brian, God has a plan. You have to trust that we'll end up where we're supposed to be at the right time."

This time Edgar was right. And that made me even angrier.

For the briefest of moments, I actually found myself missing the old days. Don't get me wrong; I knew I was meant to be away from KoRn at that point in my life, but once you've reached that level of success, starting over can be really brutal.

Of course it didn't help that right about that same time, KoRn was getting ready to release their *Untitled* album, and thanks to a massive launch campaign, it seemed like everywhere I looked, there was KoRn. Posters, billboards, magazine ads—you name it. It made me feel many mixed emotions. On top of that, they had hundreds of thousands of dollars to help them get their music out everywhere, and I couldn't even get a label to back me.

Then one day it all hit the fan. Edgar, Rodrigo, and I were in the studio working on a song, and it wasn't going well. It wasn't any one person's fault, but I still blamed them for everything. There were just too many cooks in the kitchen, and we weren't getting the sounds the song needed. Anyway, out of frustration I totally lost it . . . again.

"What are you guys doing?! I mean seriously. This all sounds like a bunch of amateurs recording a crappy demo! I thought you guys knew what you were doing!" I screamed.

"Brian, there's no reason to insult us, man. You need to chill out," Edgar shot back.

"Whatever, dude. See ya, I'm done." After exploding on Edgar and Rodrigo, I got in my car and took off as Edgar tried to stop me.

That's when I saw it—a gigantic billboard of the other guitarist in KoRn, Munky, chopping his own head off with his guitar. I'm not gonna lie, it looked freakishly cool.

Which made me even angrier, considering the mood I was in. I was ready to snap.

Back then, when I would lose control over my emotions, I'd always sink into a dark place for a while afterward. Anger, depression, and isolation would rule my life for days or weeks, and this latest episode was no exception.

A few days later I was driving with Jennea to a speaking engagement that Edgar had set up for about fifty guys who had recently gotten out of prison. They were going through a rehabilitation process, and the organization was bringing me in to tell the story of how God had turned my life around. Unfortunately I was still on edge from the studio meltdown, and I really didn't feel like speaking to *anyone* about how God had made my life better. As far as I was concerned, at that particular moment my life was miserable. My solo album wasn't going anywhere. I couldn't stand the sound of my own vocals. And we'd just blown our third label deal.

As usual, it was all or nothing with me. When things were going well, like when I took Jennea to the movie premiere, I'd experience an extreme high and feel unbelievably happy. But when things would get very difficult and confusing, I'd sometimes swing the other way and fall into a deep, dark emotional pit. I often wondered if I might have a mild case of bipolar disorder, but I never had myself checked out for that.

Edgar and I had agreed to meet the organizer for lunch before the speaking event, and as we were on our way to the restaurant, a guy cut me off on the highway. That was it—the straw that broke this camel's back. All I saw was *red*, and it completely pushed me over the edge. By the time I pulled into the parking lot, my rage level was at a nine out of ten. Then something happened that brought my rage level up to a solid ten. As I was walking around to the passenger side to get Jennea, I dropped my iPhone.

I thought I heard the screen shatter. That's when I totally lost it.

I screamed so loud with everything in me that I'm surprised traffic didn't stop. I felt like I was possessed. I picked up my phone and in a fit of rage threw it as hard as I could toward my car. It hit Jennea right in the leg, and she screamed and started crying. She wasn't seriously hurt, but I felt so horrible. Unfortunately my rage was so intense that I didn't have the strength to shift gears and comfort my little girl.

Jennea cried uncontrollably, holding her leg. "Ouch, Dad, that hurt! Why did you throw that at me? Ouch!"

I wanted to jump out of my skin and run away.

"Jennea, I didn't throw it at you. I'm sorry. It was an accident. Come on. Let's go inside." *Yeah . . . way to provide a little comfort there, Brian.*

I wished I were dead at that moment because I almost couldn't handle the weight of emotional turmoil I'd been battling for the last few days since the label letdown and studio meltdown. I had to pull it together, though, because the organizer of the event was inside the restaurant with Edgar, waiting for me. So I did what I could to calm Jennea down, put on a fake smile, and went inside. As we talked about the event, I tried to escape my reality by stuffing my face with junk food. All that did was make me feel even more sick to my stomach.

This is gonna be a disaster, I thought. And for the first time in a long time, I was right.

When we finally got to the event, most of the guys were excited to see me, but some were giving me hard looks, and hard looks were the last thing I needed at that moment. I shook a few hands and stared back at a few guys until they called me to speak. By the time I took the stage, I was so stressed out by the combination of the guy cutting me off, the iPhone, and the handful of guys still giving me the stink-eye that I was ready to lose it once and for all. Here I was, getting ready to talk about how wonderful and amazing God was, and all I could feel was anger toward him, myself, and pretty much everyone else.

I bit my tongue, grabbed the microphone, conjured up every bit of strength I could, and then, right there in front of a room full of hardened ex-cons, I broke down and cried.

The only words I could manage to say through my tears were "I love Jesus."

As soon as I choked that out, all the guys erupted in applause. Maybe they figured I was going through some intense spiritual experience at the moment, I don't know. Well, technically, I was. It just wasn't what they thought.

Edgar stared at me, wide-eyed, wondering what was wrong with me, and Jennea tried to comfort me by grabbing my hand and asking if I was okay. She was such a sweetie—even after the phone incident.

I grabbed Jennea's hand, stepped down off the stage, and walked out. I was broken into pieces. I couldn't believe I had started weeping in front of all those dudes, especially the ones giving me the hard looks. I was utterly crushed. No matter how hard I tried, my mood swings weren't getting any better, and even God didn't seem to be helping.

I'm done, I said to myself. *I quit.*

And that's exactly what I did.

As I was driving home, I mumbled under my breath so Jennea wouldn't hear me. "Jesus, I am done talking to you. If you want to do something with my life, you're gonna have to really do something major because I quit. You won't be hearing from me anymore."

I couldn't think about all the incredible things I had experienced with God during the previous couple of years. I didn't even feel thankful for his deliverance from some of the hellacious addictions of my past life. I felt like a failure as a father, a musician, and a man, and I couldn't understand how or why a loving God would play around with my life by presenting me with things so real I could almost touch them, only to take them away just as I was about to reach out and grab them. It seemed cruel.

To say I was confused would have been the understatement of the year. My mind wouldn't stop spinning from me trying to figure out what was happening to my life. I couldn't wrap my head around why I kept losing control and falling into these dark depressions. They hit around four or five times a year and usually only lasted about a week or two at the most—but when they hit, they hit hard.

I was miserable. I felt like I didn't know where I belonged in the world anymore. And that, more than anything else, may have fueled my outbursts and my depression the most.

Deep down I knew God was real, and I knew that going through hardship helped build inner strength. But once I had fallen into the pit of despair, the darkness blocked everything else out until I couldn't see, feel, or remember anything good.

So I quit talking to God. In fact, I quit talking altogether. I said a few words to Jennea every day, but that was it. I just needed to be silent.

"Jennea," I explained as gently as I could. "I need to take a break from everything for a little while. I'll take care of you, but I'm going to be really, really quiet. It has absolutely nothing to do with you. I'm just going through something with God right now that I need to work out, okay?"

It was a lot to lay on an eight-year-old, but in classic Jennea fashion, she handled the whole thing better than I did.

"Okay," she said matter-of-factly. "What are you gonna do?"

"Nothing, Nea. I'm just gonna do nothing for a while," I responded.

That *nothing* lasted for about three weeks.

True to my word, I didn't talk to God. I blocked out everyone except Jennea. I stopped answering e-mails, I turned my phone off, and I disappeared. All I did was TiVo shows and watch TV all day and all night while I lay on my couch wrapped in a blanket. Television became my new drug of choice. I watched the most intense shows available—shows about real-life murder mysteries, homicide police unit shows, reality addiction shows—in other words, pure garbage. But it made me forget about my life, and I loved that.

Day after day, from morning until bedtime, that's all I did. I never grew tired of the shows either. I was totally disturbed, yet totally captivated by all the stories about scandalous murders, rape, torture, prison, and grief. I couldn't get enough of it. It was like I was living the drama along with the people in the shows, and I was completely disconnected from the frustrations of my own life.

As the first week passed, I communicated a little more with Jennea. The second week, even more than the first, but I still hadn't uttered one word to God. I was committed. I wasn't going to do anything with my life unless Jesus made the first move.

Then, about three weeks in, there was a knock at my front door.

I was annoyed because I was in the middle of a great murder story. *Who in the world is knocking on my door without calling first? What is it about the two stone walls and an electric gate out front that says, "Hey, I'll bet this guy loves unexpected visitors. Let's pop in and say hi!"* I pushed Pause on the TiVo and slowly snuck over to the window.

Edgar. *Perfect.*

I rolled my eyes, took a deep breath, and opened the front door.

"Bro, where have you been?" he asked. "We've been worried about you. We've been trying to call and e-mail you for weeks. We thought you were dead. What's going on?"

"Look, man," I explained, "I can't handle all these ups and downs. I don't know what I want to do with my life. I feel like I don't even know God at all." I shook my head and sighed. "Man, I don't know what to believe anymore."

Then Edgar said something completely unexpected.

"Bro, Ryko called back. They changed their mind. They want to do the deal with us."

Whoa.

Out of nowhere, I felt an inner light of hope ignite, and a tiny, tiny smile started to form that, hard as I tried, I couldn't stop. This was it. Jesus was using Edgar's visit to make the first move and offer me a hand out of my dark, shadowy cave.

Edgar filled me in on the details, and we agreed to meet up in a few days. After he left, I went back to the couch and unpaused the TV. But within a few minutes, I felt something stirring inside of me. I re-hit Pause, walked into my bedroom, and closed the door.

God, I miss you. I don't understand what you're doing with me. I'm so tired. Why are things the way they are? Why can't I get past all these mood swings and bouts of anger and depression? What should I do? Where do I even go from here? I feel you calling me back to you, but I'm stuck on this TV addiction. Please take it all away from me, in Jesus' name.

The next day I took Jennea to school and came back home to settle in on the couch for another full day of televised crime, death, and drama, but something was different. I just couldn't get into the stories. I switched over to a show about a murder in Mississippi, and as the narrator described the crime scene over some grisly video footage, I suddenly started feeling nauseous. I kept trying to watch, but the feeling got worse, so I deleted all the gruesome shows I had recorded.

And just like that, I went back to my normal life.

Once again, God raised me up after living like a dead man.

I spent the next few days making up for lost time with Jennea. It was beautiful out, so I took her and a friend to a water park. I knew they'd love that, and frankly, it wouldn't kill me to get out of the house after being glued to the couch for so long. Jennea and her friend loved going down the slides. I even went down a few times myself. We were all having a blast until the water park staff had to clear the whole wave pool because some kid took a dump in the water. Occupational hazard, I guess . . .

A few weeks earlier something like that would've sent me right over the edge, but that day I was full of positive energy. So instead of flipping out, I got out of the water (as fast as humanly possible), grabbed a beach chair, and settled in to do a little reading.

As it happens, an amazing book had fallen into my hands a few days earlier. It was called *God Meant It for Good* by R. T. Kendall. I saw it online and knew in my heart that I needed to read it, so I ordered a copy. It was all about Joseph, who was forced into slavery and thrown into prison. Then he was elevated and honored, only to be thrown back into prison and then elevated and honored again. Up, then down, then up, then down again.

Man! It all sounded so similar to what I'd been going through. Almost signing with a label, then losing the deal. Gaining a new label, then losing that one. My emotional up-and-down roller-coaster rides. That book was like Gatorade for an extremely thirsty soul, and I drank in every word. The trials that Joseph had to endure were far worse than anything I had been going through, and yet through it all he never once wavered in his faith—never once! He understood everything that happened to him was part of the divine plan to prepare him for greatness. So instead of getting mired in depression or self-pity (like yours truly), Joseph viewed every setback as an opportunity to grow closer to God and to let his power strengthen him. Me? I wasn't quite there yet. But I wanted to be.

That book was an eye-opener for me. Joseph's story is positive proof that God can take any situation, no matter how awful, and use it for good. Case in point—were it not for a little kid pooping in a pool, I might never have learned one of the greatest spiritual lessons of my life.

Just sayin'.

A few days after taking the girls to the water park, I drove down to the studio to meet with Edgar about setting some possible dates to start recording again. We were laser-focused . . . for about twenty minutes. Then somehow Edgar shifted the conversation away from music and onto a new idea he had.

He wanted to start a meat delivery business, and he wanted to make me his partner. Yeah, you read that right. He made it sound really good though. He even wanted to give all the profits away to help orphans. According to Edgar, all we needed to get started were a couple of vans, which he'd already picked out. Since I was his partner, he asked if I'd go with him to pick them up. Not so sure how I felt about starting a meat business but 100 percent sold on the idea of raising money for orphans, I agreed, and off we went.

When we got to the Chevy dealership, Edgar pointed out the two vans he wanted and the salesman started pulling together the paperwork. I was on my phone checking my e-mail when Edgar called me over.

"You gotta sign the papers, bro," he said.

"What papers?" I asked.

"The papers for the vans for the meat business," he answered.

Wait . . . What?

Edgar didn't tell me he was taking me to the dealer to purchase two new vehicles in *my* name.

"Bro, we talked about this at the studio," he explained.

We did? I quickly replayed the conversation in my head, but Edgar mentioning this was not on my mind's playback. Nevertheless, I ended up signing the paperwork, and twenty minutes later I was the proud— albeit slightly confused—owner of two brand-new Chevy vans. Not to mention co-owner of a meat delivery business. That made a lot of sense . . .

Actually, very little about Edgar's and my business dealings made a lot of sense. He would sit me down and tell me all kinds of great things about us becoming partners in different businesses. He named me president of one company, a senior executive whatever of another, and CEO of a third. Edgar made it sound as though I was becoming a successful businessman just by being in partnership with him. He was playing me hard, and I didn't even realize it.

And I wasn't the only one. Edgar had a family member who owned some property on the East Coast as well as a prime piece of land overseas, and he convinced that person to sell it and invest the money in our companies. Frankly, it made me feel a little better knowing that there was someone besides me contributing large sums of cash into our businesses.

I should point out that all the money I gave the businesses was given at my sole discretion. I wasn't coerced into anything. I know what you must be thinking. *Why on earth would you give your money to someone like Edgar to oversee?* The answer is simple: I trusted him (in the beginning). But that wasn't the only reason.

After I hit the big time with KoRn, I became obsessed with money. I believed in it and trusted in it more than anyone or anything. But after my encounter with Jesus, all I wanted to do was separate myself from everything negative about the entertainment industry, and money was a huge part of that. I had watched money turn incredibly humble people into greedy, power-hungry egomaniacs—myself included—and it really made me sick.

So part of me was trying to get rid of my money by putting it into our businesses in hopes that it would grow and help feed orphans. In my mind, handing over control of my money was my way of walking by faith and not trusting in the almighty dollar like I used to.

Technically a lot of my money did go into recording my solo album, so it wasn't like it was all wasted. It was just totally mismanaged.

Despite all his faults, I have to admit Edgar was always very up front about his past. For example, a few years earlier he had gotten into a disagreement with a former business partner, and as a result he had a couple of lawsuits hanging over his head. Of course he always explained it to me in a way that made it sound like the other guy was delusional and that the lawsuits were some kind of "spiritual attack."

At any rate, those lawsuits kept Edgar from being able to put houses, bank accounts, or businesses in his own name. Instead, one of Edgar's family members—or, as it turns out, me—would put everything in their name, and Edgar would help run all the businesses from behind the scenes. At one point I even took out a line of credit with one of Edgar's family members to help support the businesses.

I honestly had no clue what Edgar was doing. I just left everything to him, stayed out of the day-to-day stuff, and only got involved when he needed my signature on something.

And he needed my signature a lot.

Over the course of the next several months, he made me president or CEO of about a half-dozen companies, even though I was never involved in running them and had no idea how they worked. All I did was sign my name. And that ended up getting me in a lot of trouble.

Shortly after we—sorry, I—bought the vans, Edgar was subpoenaed into court by one of his former business partners who was suing him for millions of dollars. Naturally, Edgar strongly proclaimed his innocence.

"It's the weirdest thing, bro," he explained. "I was partners with this guy, and all of a sudden he accused me of stealing all this money. It's so insane."

"Why would he be coming after you so ruthlessly?" I asked. "Did you take anything from him?"

"I've done a lot of bad things in the past, Brian," he assured me, "but I swear I didn't do what this guy is accusing me of."

I didn't know what to think, but my suspicions sure were beginning to surface. As I've said, Edgar always blamed his troubles on a spiritual attack, so much so that we used to joke that he was like Paul in the Bible, who kept getting dragged into court even though he was innocent.

I went to court a couple of times to support Edgar during the suit against him, and it was intense. They accused him of some serious stuff—embezzlement, fraud, hiding funds, cover-ups. It was bad.

What really blew me away was when the guy told the judge how Edgar not only destroyed his family but that the financial ruin he caused made his dad suffer so much grief that it actually led to his death. I thought, *If this really is a spiritual attack, it's the most convincing one I've ever seen!*

It kept getting worse for Edgar.

After the guy finished his testimony, the judge brought the hammer down on Edgar. He said Edgar had to pay somewhere around a couple hundred thousand dollars immediately, and if he couldn't come up with the money by three o'clock that afternoon, Edgar was going to jail.

Fortunately for him, Edgar's family wrote the judge a check, and he was able to beat jail time by the skin of his teeth.

It was all so confusing. On the one hand I knew Edgar had a shady past. But it was wild hearing this guy rip Edgar to shreds in court and talk about how he ruined his whole life. Yet Edgar was always so sure of himself, and a lot of times he showed such an incredible love for Jesus and others. He really did seem to be the real deal. In fact, throughout that entire court case, even though the threat of going to jail was always there, the only thing Edgar would say was, "If I get sent to jail, it must mean someone in jail needs Jesus because that's the only reason I'll be going if I do."

I didn't know what to think. Then things got worse.

The next afternoon I was walking into the studio and I heard someone call my name from just beyond the locked gate.

"Mr. Welch?" the guy said.

I could tell by the tone of his voice that it was bad news, so I decided to ignore him. I kept walking, and he kept talking.

"Mr. Welch, you have been served," the guy said, dropping an envelope full of papers through the locked gate. Edgar was being sued by yet another company, and this time they were going after me too.

What the . . . ? Why are they bringing me into this?

It was bad enough that these people were calling Edgar a crook, but now they were calling me one, and accusing me of hiding information to protect Edgar. It was completely nuts. Frustrated and confused, I decided to confront him.

"Edgar, why am I involved in all this trash from your past?"

"Brian, I'm really sorry, man. I know this seems like a disaster, but it won't be a big deal," he promised. "I'll have a lawyer there with you, and he'll help you through it."

That was both comforting and unsettling at the same time. On the upside Edgar really did seem to feel bad, and he did get me a lawyer. Not that it helped much. The plaintiff's lawyer was brutal, and he came after me with everything but the kitchen sink.

"Mr. Welch, are you aware that Edgar may be hiding funds in order to defraud our client?"

"No," I answered.

"Isn't it true that you and one of Edgar's family members became business partners for the sole purpose of hiding Edgar's involvement as the real CEO?" he pressed.

"No," I said. "I don't know about any of that. I'm only an artist. I'm not involved with the business side of things."

"Then why is your name on the corporate documents?" he sternly asked.

"Well, I, um . . . it's just complicated," I mumbled, actually not knowing the answer myself.

"Are you currently hiding money under your name to help Edgar defraud our client?"

"No way," I shot back. "I've never done anything like that in my life."

He went on and on and on. He accused me of being crooked for so long that it started to feel like I *was* guilty. I was terrified that if I accidentally said the wrong thing, I would get busted for something I didn't do. Granted, I did have a lawyer there with me, but I didn't feel like he was doing much to help. In fact, he seemed scared of them too. It was a nightmare.

So what did I do? I did what I always did in these situations. I made things even worse.

As if money wasn't flying out of my bank accounts fast enough, thanks to all Edgar's legal fees, for some reason I decided this was the ideal time to trade in my Dodge Magnum for a BMW. In my defense, that was one sick car. It was jet black with twenty-two-inch chrome rims and dark, tinted windows.

Back in the KoRn days, we would always have our business manager weigh in on all our major purchases to make sure everything was on the up-and-up. Well, guess who I brought with me to the dealership that day? Yep. Edgar. Long story short, I ended up getting in *way* over my head with the BMW, digging an even bigger ditch to bury myself in.

For those of you keeping score, I now had two mortgage payments, a huge line of credit out in my name, monthly payments on two Chevy vans, and now a massive car payment of my own. There were thousands of dollars going out every month, yet despite the fact that I was president and CEO of a bunch of different companies, there was hardly anything coming in.

Then, out of nowhere, something good actually happened.

Toward the end of that year, I received a forty-thousand-dollar check from KoRn's business manager for publishing rights.

When you're hemorrhaging cash and you receive a nice-sized check in the mail, the smart thing to do would be to put it away, but as we've already established, I was pretty much a first-class idiot back then. Up until that point, I had always given my money to Edgar voluntarily. But now we were having some serious cash-flow problems, so as soon as Edgar found out about the check and before I could do anything stupid like put it in savings or use it to help make my mortgage payments, he hit me up for a loan.

And—you guessed it—Idiot Boy said, "Okay."

Some people might say I was being brainwashed, or say, "See what religion does to people?" But I wasn't about to blame religion—or even Edgar—for *my* decisions. This was my journey, and I had to walk through all of this in order to learn some important lessons.

In the meantime, though, I decided to give Edgar the loan because he promised to reimburse me in a short amount of time. We even signed an agreement, which we'd never done before. But more than that, I did it because there were other people involved. You see, Edgar had hired a bunch of employees down at the meat plant, and he was more than a week behind on payroll. We were heading into the holidays, and I didn't want to see a bunch of innocent people have a horrible Christmas. So I gave him the loan to cover the payroll. I may have been an idiot, but I was an idiot with a good heart.

For the next few weeks, everything was relatively calm. Jennea was almost finished with school for the holidays, the guinea pigs were still happy and accounted for, and for the moment Edgar's legal problems seemed to be taking a break.

Then one day while I was just hanging out at the house, I got a call from Archie, one of the other artists Edgar was working with. And he didn't sound happy.

"Bro, you have to get down here," he said. "You will not believe what's going on."

He was right. I couldn't believe it.

Our recording studio was being invaded by a Mexican television news team who specialized in investigative reports, and—surprise, surprise—they were looking for Edgar.

Seriously? I thought. *Am I being filmed for an episode of Punk'd or something?* I thought for sure Ashton Kutcher was going to come busting through my door any minute, laughing at me. But believe me, nobody was laughing.

Edgar had been accused of hiring unsuspecting Mexican workers and then cheating them out of pay. Apparently this kind of thing had been happening a lot around the Phoenix area, and the Mexican news channel was cracking down on it. I wanted to believe there wasn't any truth to it, but since I had just given Edgar a massive loan to bankroll all the workers that he had stiffed down at the meat plant, it was hard to make a case in his favor.

A few days later the news team went to the meat plant, and all the employees that Edgar had hired were outside picketing. They had signs with Edgar's name on them, and the news team was broadcasting live, interviewing disgruntled employees. It was unbelievable. Everything was falling apart.

So what did Edgar do?

He bolted.

"Brian, we're under attack," he told me over the phone. "But God is with us and will see us through this. I'm gonna take off and talk to some potential investors," he continued. "Trust me, Brian, a miracle is coming."

And then just like that he was gone.

As president, senior executive, and CEO, I was left holding the bag.

Or should I say, bags.

I started to panic. I finally had to face the truth about Edgar's character, and it wasn't pretty. I felt like a complete idiot. My mind was racing.

How could I let myself get caught up in all this? What about my album? What about my daughter? How are we going to live? I had millions of dollars three years ago, and now this? Will we have to move in with my parents?

I don't know how I didn't fall into one of my massively depressed, angry-isolation episodes at this point. Perhaps it was because everything was spinning out of control so fast that my adrenaline kicked in. Who knows? All I could do was ask the Lord for massive help. Despite all my doubts and fears, I knew he would do something. He always came through for me, and I needed him badly now.

Lord, I've made a lot of mistakes with finances over the last few years, but I've given my entire life over to you. Things are crashing down all around me in every possible way, but I know you will see me through it. I've learned that my real life is hidden with you in spirit, above every negative circumstance. I'm trying to keep my peace, but I can't do it without you. It doesn't work on my own. I love you so much. Help me. Please.

As usual, he did not disappoint.

A few days after the Mexican news team raided the studio, I got a call from Gary, one of the guys who worked at the studio. Like me, Gary had also been taken in by Edgar. But unlike me, Gary had a much clearer picture of everything Edgar had been up to, and it wasn't good.

"Brian, Edgar is really in a bad spot, and he's not going to get out of this one," Gary explained.

"Yeah," I agreed. "I can see things are falling apart."

"Listen," he continued, "you don't know the half of it. He's pretty much gone back to his old habits. Brian, I'm telling you, man, you need to cut all ties with him—*now!*"

Everything Gary said made perfect sense, but that didn't change the fact that I was legally tied to pretty much every shady deal Edgar had going.

"How am I supposed to do that?" I asked. "I'm so tied up in all this that it'll take a miracle to get me out."

Fortunately, Gary had a plan, and we started executing it immediately.

Step one: get all the masters and back-up copies of my solo album out of Edgar's house.

This part was easy. While Edgar was on the road dodging the Mexican news mafia, his parents were taking care of things at his house. I knew Edgar's parents pretty well. They were older, but his mom was still a very sharp, strong, East-Coast woman.

"Hi, Mrs. C. How are you?" I asked as Edgar's mom opened the front door.

"Hi, Brian, honey. Hi, Gary." Mrs. C. smiled back. "Come on in, boys, and sit down. How are you guys doing?"

Wow. How do you answer that?

"You know," she continued, "Edgar still plans to keep everything going, but this sure has been a wild ride, what with the meat plant and the fiasco with the news station, hasn't it?"

"Yeah, it has," I said, trying to stay upbeat. I really did like Edgar's mom. "I'm sure everything will work out though."

"Would you boys like something to drink?" I could sense she was starting to feel a little uncomfortable, and frankly so were we. We just wanted to get those masters and get out of there.

"No, thank you," I declined politely. "We just need to pick up some hard drives, so I can start working on my music again."

"Okay, sweetie," she said, standing up. "Follow me. Edgar keeps all his recording materials in the hall closet."

I have to admit, I felt a little bad—almost like I was stealing something from her. But they were my masters and I had paid for them. I figured it was about time I got something out of all this. So Gary and I grabbed the masters and split.

Step one—done.

Step two: start our own label and build a team.

About a month before he bolted, Edgar had hired a guy named

Carl to help get the distribution deal finished with Ryko. As soon as we got my masters out of Edgar's house, Gary and I arranged to meet with Carl to fill him in on everything that had been going on.

"Carl, we found out about a few things that have been going on with Edgar, and we've decided to part ways with him and start our own label," Gary said.

"Yeah," I continued, "and we were wondering if you'd like to come on board with us and see if we can still work out a deal with Ryko."

Oddly enough, Carl didn't seem the least bit surprised.

"Well, I can't tell you that it's a total shock," he answered. "That guy has been all over the place since I met him."

"Yeah," Gary agreed. "It's just better this way."

Carl sat back in his chair and stared at us both for a few seconds. Then he said the words we were hoping to hear.

"Okay, I'm in. But it won't be easy to tell Ryko about this," he cautioned. "It's gonna look pretty unprofessional. But I guess all we can do is try. I'll give the guys a call tomorrow and see what I can do."

Step two—done.

Step three: come up with a name for the label.

Our old record label name was tied to Edgar, so Carl, Gary, and I started brainstorming new names. E-mails flew back and forth for days, but nothing seemed to stick. We weren't having any luck, so I decided to throw it out to God, and once again he delivered.

That night I had a vivid dream that Gary got into my car and started driving me somewhere. Where, I can't remember, but we were definitely driving somewhere—and fast. So when Gary came over the next day, I told him about the dream, and he said, "Why don't we call it Drive or Driven or something like that?"

"Yeah, I like that!" I answered.

We went with Driven Music Group.

It had a nice ring to it.

A few days later, Carl put some artwork together, got us a logo, and we were off.

Step three—done.

Now all we needed was a distributor.

If you ever find yourself dealing with a record label, there's one thing you should know: they are never in a hurry to get anything done. You have to be very patient. Carl and Gary had been in regular communication with Ryko for months, but the company was hesitant to move forward because of the whole Edgar situation. That was understandable. It must have seemed pretty shady.

Thankfully, they believed in me, and they liked the business plan Gary and Carl had put together. Finally, after months of going non-stop back and forth, I ended up signing the distribution deal I'd been waiting years for.

Lord, you are such a trip sometimes. Just when so many crushing disappointments come crashing down on me and I get stripped of everything, here you come dropping down an awesome encouragement. Thanks for all of this. You're so awesome. In Jesus' name, let this company be a success for my friends and me!

It seemed like I'd been working on my solo album forever, and now the time had finally come. It was a chance to begin again. All of us were super excited. We didn't know what the future held exactly, but our expectations were high. Like a racehorse out of the gate, we were off and running at full speed, *Driven* by our desire to succeed.

After everything I'd been through, I was finally looking forward to some smooth sailing. But even though Edgar had vanished, the problems he created remained. And I was still tied to all of them.

CHAPTER 4

―――――――――――――――――――――――――――――

HEAVEN AND HELL

Feeling the euphoria of success and the sting of failure at the same time is one of the most peculiar experiences you can have. But that's exactly what I stepped into in 2008 as my solo career started to launch and my material life continued to crumble.

After Gary, Carl, and I signed the incorporation papers for Driven Music Group and the distribution agreements with Ryko, we were officially ready to go. Carl already rented a building unit in a nice business district, so we decided to move Driven in with him and set up shop. There was only enough room for two offices, so Carl and Gary took those, and I just came by as needed to go over things. This may come as a surprise, but I've never really been a nine-to-five sort of a guy.

By that time I had pretty much conquered my vocal fears, and I had finally learned what kind of recording style worked best for me. I like to call it "recording myself without anyone else in the room." There's just something about recording vocal tracks that makes me go insane. You see, I have a gift that can seemingly turn on itself and become a curse. The gift part is that I have a great ear. I can hear notes and how they blend together really well. The curse part is that my brain has difficulty telling my mouth what note to hit as I'm singing. As a result, when I hear the music coming through the headphones, I have a difficult time making my voice do what my brain wants it to do.

Every time I record my own vocals in a studio, I get all anxious and sweat like a pig because I feel like I'm going to butcher every line before I even try to sing it. It's brutal. And that's even when I'm recording by myself. Now imagine me trying to sing with a producer and an engineer listening to every note that comes out of my mouth. Totally out of the question for me. No can do.

So how did I finally manage to lay down my vocal tracks?

Simple. I recorded them in a separate studio on the opposite end of the building through my own personal computer using GarageBand. Ironic, right? Thousands of dollars' worth of fancy equipment at my fingertips, and I launch my solo career using a free app that you can download on any iPhone.

After I laid down my vocals, Rodrigo would do his thing to get the best sound quality out of it as he possibly could. It's an odd way to record, but Rodrigo had a lot of expensive cables, filters, and programs he could run my tracks through, and by the time he was done, it sounded pretty good. Not great, but good enough. Plus, it kept me from tearing studios apart and driving off into the sunset like a deranged maniac. Once I fell into my groove, I had all the vocals completed in a few weeks.

When all the tracks were ready, it was time to start mixing the rest of the songs. For those of you who don't know, mixing is the process where an engineer mixes all the different instrumental and vocal tracks together to make the final song sound as good as possible. When it goes well, songs come out sounding better than you ever imagined.

The first step was to find a good mixer in Arizona who we could afford. We ended up connecting with a guy named Ralph Patlan, who was extremely talented. Ralph and I worked day and night for weeks, and even though it took a long time and cost a pretty penny, it was a great experience. Ralph made the songs sound way better than I ever expected, and after all the crazy setbacks and delays, it was exciting to finally hear the finished product.

Lord, this is amazing! I've been waiting so long to hear my music sound like this! Lately everything with my album and label is going so positively. I can't wait to see what you do next!

Man, did I treasure the times when things were going great and my depression wasn't ruining me.

After the mixing was done, we hired a guy to take some new publicity photos, and these were way better than the photos Edgar and I did in Croatia. No more creepy pedophile-looking shots. We also came up with a really cool piece of art for the CD cover: a black and sepia-toned image of me all broken and beat up with an angel behind me—an awesome symbol of my freedom. I decided on the album title *Save Me from Myself,* the same name as my first book.

The next order of business was to choose the first single. We decided to go with "Flush," a song about overcoming drug and alcohol abuse. It just seemed fitting. Then we updated all my websites, selected a release date, hired a publicist, and shot a music video.

To be honest, the video was kind of crazy. It started off with me in a straitjacket connected to a bunch of chains, struggling to break free. That part worked. But then we cut to all these girls in bikinis playing with pink sand that was supposed to symbolize meth. They played with it, licked it, and poured it all over each other. Then they all started vomiting black tar and died, and the video ended with them all breaking free from their body bags. The concept was cool, but I think it went overboard a bit, especially where the girls were concerned. I mean, they were directed to do a bunch of crazy, sexy shots while a room full of guys just stood around, watching the filming. I was like, *What is going on right now?* That wasn't what I was going for.

After we finished the video, I told Gary and Carl that I was uncomfortable with some of the scenes, but they thought I should be real and tell it like it was because that's what my past life was all about. So we left it as-is, but I did get quite a bit of backlash from it. If we were to shoot that video over today, I would go in a completely different direction. But back then, let's just say it seemed like a good idea at the time.

At one point I even sat Jennea down, showed her the video, and explained what it all meant, especially the part about how different my life today is compared to when I was strung out on meth. Yeah, it was uncomfortable, but I didn't want some kid from school to say anything to her about it without letting her hear my take first. As young as she was, I think she understood my heart about the whole thing, but not surprisingly, she didn't like the video either.

Meth. It always did get me into trouble.

Aside from the slight misstep on the video, everything else leading up to the launch of the album went great. It had been so long since I released a record that everything felt brand-new to me—especially since I was sober this time around.

—

I never heard from Edgar again. I did, however, hear from a bunch of guys Edgar had allegedly cheated financially, and they were thrilled to hear about Driven and the upcoming launch—just not for the same reasons I was.

"Listen, Brian," said the latest in a seemingly endless string of angry voices I'd heard over the phone that month, "you were in the room when we discussed all of this, remember? We were all backstage at the *Last Call with Carson Daly* show, and we talked about how we gave you guys money for your solo album. We looked you in the eye and told you we were going to help you, so the way we figure it, we're entitled to a share of Driven as well as whatever you make off of your album."

I felt bad, but these guys hadn't given Edgar money specifically for my album. There were other projects Edgar brought them into as well. The main problem was, I wasn't there when this whole deal actually went down.

"Listen. I'm sorry this is happening, but I wasn't even there when you guys discussed everything," I explained. "You discussed all the finances with Edgar, not me. If Edgar made promises to you, I had nothing to do with it." Then I said something that wasn't necessarily the truth. "Edgar should be back in town any day now. I can't help you, but as soon as he gets back from his business trip, I'm sure he'll be able to settle everything."

I didn't really believe any of that, but it seemed to calm the guy down. At least for the time being, that problem was solved. But there were plenty more where that came from.

A few days after the phone confrontation, I was sitting at home watching TV (no murderous shows) when I heard a knock at my front door. I had a sinking feeling in the pit of my stomach. The last time someone had knocked on my door in the middle of the day, it was Edgar.

I should have had those walls electrified.

I quietly made my way toward the window and peeked out to see who it was. I didn't recognize the guy. It was some dude in plain clothes carrying an envelope, so I slipped back behind the curtain. After he knocked a couple more times, he walked away.

Huh. So much for that.

After he left, I went back to watching TV for about half an hour or so, then I headed to the garage and got into my car to run some errands. I hit the garage door opener, started backing up, and then quickly slammed on the brakes. That same guy was just standing there in my driveway.

What the heck? Who is this guy?

Then he walked over to the driver's side window, dropped the envelope on my windshield, and said, "Mr. Welch, you have been served."

I couldn't believe it. Another lawsuit!

I felt like getting out of my car, chasing the idiot down, and breaking his hands, but that probably would've resulted in another lawsuit, and I was already over my quota for the month. I just rolled down my window, grabbed the envelope, tossed it into the backseat, and took off to run my errands. When I got back, I noticed a handwritten note stuck to my mailbox. It was from Ross Robinson, who had produced the first two KoRn albums.

Hey dude,

I'm in town for Wes Borland's [Limp Bizkit] wedding, and someone gave me your address. I want to see you and catch up.

Seriously, is there a sign out front that says Visitors Welcome?

Almost ten years had passed since KoRn worked with Ross, but KoRn had hired him to produce their new album that year, and I knew exactly what he was up to. He wanted me to be involved with KoRn's latest album he was producing, but I wanted nothing to do with it.

Later that day I was watching TV again when there was another knock at the front door. It was Ross. He'd jumped my fences.

Man, I even locked the gate this time.

This dude was persistent. He kept knocking and knocking, but I just ignored him, and eventually he gave up. I love the dude, but at that time in my life I had no desire to talk about KoRn.

What next? I thought.

It turned out, Chevy was next. Since Edgar had fallen behind on the van payments and the meat delivery business was currently under siege by the Mexican news mafia, the good people at Chevy wanted my head on a platter. Shortly after they started calling and sending me notices, I talked to Gary, and he helped me put some ads for the vans on Craigslist. I wasn't holding out a lot of hope. After all, how many people could there possibly be in the Phoenix area who were in the market for a used van that smelled like raw meat, let alone two? And yet, surprisingly, we managed to find a buyer for one of them, and one was better than none. The guy purchased the van for around $10,000, which I immediately handed over to Chevrolet. Now we just had to find a buyer for the second one. One week passed, and then another, and still no buyer. So about a week later for the first time in my life, I watched as a tow truck came and repossessed a vehicle from my residence. Talk about the sting of failure. I felt like a loser.

I tried to keep everything that was happening from Jennea, but between me being stressed out, all the heated phone calls, and now tow trucks coming around, I finally had to come clean.

"Jennea, Edgar and I have parted ways," I explained. "So a lot of things are changing right now."

"Why? What did he do?" Luckily for me, she seemed only mildly interested.

"Well, he just has some things he needs to work on, so Gary, Carl, and I are gonna do our own thing from now on."

It didn't explain much, but then there wasn't much about what was happening that I could explain myself. There was one thing I was sure of, though, and I wanted to make sure Jennea knew it too.

"There are some people we got into arguments with over business stuff, so you might hear some conversations about that, but don't worry, Jesus is gonna take care of us, just like he always has."

In spite of everything that was happening, I knew without a doubt that God was going to turn it all around. It may have taken my eyes a while to open up to what a piece of work Edgar was, but I never once doubted God's ability to fix every disaster that came—whether it was my fault or not.

On the surface I may have felt fear and anxiety, but deep down I had a peace that I naturally shouldn't have had. I was steadfast in my belief that God was up to something good—even when everything seemed to be falling apart.

Right around the time the van got repossessed, I had the most mind-blowing encounter with Jesus I'd ever had. I genuinely believe God gave me this encounter so I would know he was still there, and so that I would have the strength to deal with all the catastrophes happening and those still to come. For those of you who don't believe in this stuff, trust me, you will believe in it the moment your heart stops beating if you don't figure it out before then. It's more *real* than the air you breathe.

I was sitting on the floor of my home office listening to a new CD from Kimberly and Alberto Rivera. The CD was called *Captured: Songs of Destiny from the Father*, and when the song "Captured" came on, something indescribable happened. As I was listening to the soft piano-synth music and the angelic voice of Kimberly singing the prophetic words, "You have captured my heart—I will show you great and mighty things to come," I swear to you, Jesus entered my room. I didn't see him physically, but the atmosphere in my house completely shifted as he walked into that room and stepped inside of me. I knew he already lived in me by faith, but this was a strategic visitation to strengthen and prepare me for my calling.

As Jesus mentions in John 14:21, "Whoever [really] loves Me will be loved by My Father, and I will love him and reveal Myself to him. [I will make Myself real to him]" (AMP).

Even you. But you'd have to spend the time to convince him to visit you yourself. Nobody can do that for you. We shouldn't be shocked by hearing of visitations. I personally know so many people who have had way more amazing visitations from Jesus or angels than I have. Visitations can happen to anyone who radically pursues and starts asking God for them on a continual basis.

Even *you*.

Jesus appeared to many people after he was raised from the dead. Now that the original disciples are with Christ, we who are on the earth should expect these things, too, (if we truly desire them) as we grow in intimacy with Jesus.

At that instant, the room filled with a peace so heavy and so thick—so ethereal. It kind of felt like a thousand pounds of divine peace just fell on me. It was the purest, most amazing love I'd ever felt—like an invisible river of heaven's glory poured into my house. It's impossible for mere words to fully describe. It's like the first time you fall deeply in love with someone. Your friends can't comprehend the intense butterflies and the incredible sense of euphoria that you're feeling because they aren't in love with the one you love—only you are. It's similar regarding divine encounters. It's something you have to experience for yourself to understand.

To me, believing in Christ isn't about reading the Bible, trying to be good, and following rules. It's way more amazing than that. We all have the opportunity to *share* God's divine nature firsthand (2 Peter 1:4), and that is a truth that is beyond staggering.

As I felt Jesus step inside of me, tears started pouring down my cheeks like a river. They weren't tear "drops." They were very warm tears like thick streams that didn't stop flowing. I'd never experienced tears like that in my life. As the music played, the only thing I could hear the Lord speak to my mind was, *These are my tears. You and I are one. We are no longer separate* (1 Corinthians 6:17). My body began to shake, and I was breathing very heavily like the wind got knocked out of me. I tried to breathe normally, but it was impossible. That's when I saw a faint vision of myself floating way out in the ocean, and I felt the Lord whisper, *I am giving you the oceans of my Spirit.* The revelation of how God and man can be joined into oneness through Christ became completely real to me in that moment. It was one of the most intense experiences of my entire life, and definitely the most important.

Over the years I had always asked for more visions, so when I saw myself floating in the ocean, I asked God to confirm that it was from him. About an hour later Jennea came home from a church festival with a blue stuffed bear in her arms. "Daddy, Daddy!" she yelled. "Look, I won this bear at the church today. I named him Ocean."

I about fell over laughing like a drunk man. God is so real.

The whole encounter that day was so incredible that I didn't want to experience it alone, so I asked Jesus to touch Jennea in some way. Later that night as we were driving somewhere, she asked me to turn down the stereo and, completely out of the blue, said, "Dad, I feel like I have butterflies in my stomach."

I almost drove right off the road. I looked back at her and saw that she had the cutest, most bashful, smiley face, almost like she was embarrassed about something. I explained to her that I'd prayed for Jesus to touch her and that he was doing just that right that second. She was blown away.

God, in all his loving-kindness, strengthened me with that mind-blowing encounter right when I needed it most. The experience actually ended up lasting about two weeks with other crazy cool things happening that I won't get into now, but soon it was time to get back to normal life. I had to walk by faith again, to take those experiences and reminders of God's love with me into whatever lay ahead. And let me tell you, the Edgar difficulties were only a small preview of what was coming in the not-so-distant future.

—

With no new money coming in and my account practically empty, I was having a difficult time making my first and second mortgage payments—not to mention my car and credit card payments—and my phone was ringing off the hook from bill collectors. The ship was sinking fast, and no matter how hard I tried, there was no way I could save it.

The next month I pooled all the money I had and put it toward the two mortgage payments. I couldn't lose the house. Unfortunately a couple of weeks later I realized I had nothing left in my account to buy groceries with. I actually had to tear the house apart looking for spare change in sofa cushions, the bottom of the washing machine, the floor of the car, and the pockets of all my jeans and jackets. And for two weeks I was able to buy bread, lunch meat, cheese, and eggs. I had never experienced a low like that before as an adult, but even though I was stressing out a lot, I knew it was only a test and things would eventually turn around. More important, I wanted Jennea to learn a lesson that would stay with her a lifetime about how to keep the faith and stay at peace in times of financial lack. So one evening after a very light dinner of cheese sandwiches, I sat her down and explained the situation.

"Nea, a lot of things are happening right now, and my money is kind of low," I explained gently. "But what have I always taught you about money?"

"That God gives us stuff and not to trust in money."

"That's right. And he will take care of us now, just like he always does," I said, giving her a hug. "Tell you what . . . why don't you go through all the drawers in your room, and I'll go through all my drawers and look for quarters so we can go to the grocery store."

"Okay!" she said, smiling.

"Come on, Lord," I said playfully, herding her toward her room, "show us the money!"

I was determined not to walk in fear, and even if I slipped a little in the coming days, I definitely wasn't going to let Jennea see me scared. I was determined to show Jennea how much God could be trusted to care for us in every way—especially with money. That's an area where most people struggle with trusting God. I wanted her to learn from this and carry the experience in her heart so she would remember not to totally collapse when she faced similar situations as an adult.

One day at a particularly low point, I was searching the Scriptures and praying for encouragement to help me out of my financial rut and a verse jumped out at me: "If we have enough food and clothing, let us be content" (1 Timothy 6:8 NLT).

Dang it! That's no help! I thought. *What about all those other verses that say if you give, you will receive so much more?*

We had clothes. And for the moment anyway, we had food, so I just had to dig deep inside and stay at peace. I knew God would provide. And wouldn't you know it, once again, he did just that.

Right about the time Jennea and I had unearthed every last quarter in the house, I got an e-mail from Gary. He had been talking to Carl, and somehow they found out about a bunch of KoRn royalties I was owed—almost $250,000 worth. Bam! Finally, a lifeline. I had no idea this was coming, but the timing was nothing short of miraculous. I only received a smaller payment up front with many more payments to come, but it still felt like I had won the lottery—again!

Of course, by that time I was so behind with all my bills that even if I did receive the entire $250,000 up front, that amount wasn't going to be enough to keep my head above water in the long run. It was that bad.

In the end, I decided to hold on to the money, let the house go, and move Jennea and me into a much cheaper apartment above some friends of ours. I tried for months to short sell the house, but after two prospective buyers backed out, it went into foreclosure. I was frustrated because Carl had a house that he was able to short sell, and I couldn't understand why mine didn't. But at least I was starting to see a faint sliver of light at the end of the tunnel.

The couple we moved in above, Jeremy and Roxanne, had been friends of ours for a couple of years. They had two young kids—Eden and Seth—and their daughter, Eden, was a little younger than Jennea, so they hung out a lot. When I told Jennea about the move, she was actually excited.

Still, we almost didn't get the place.

Since my credit was so bad, Jeremy had to call the management company and talk them into letting me rent it. They agreed to do it if I would give them a few months' rent up front, which my first KoRn payment covered. We ended up moving half of our belongings into the apartment and the other half into a storage unit. Not one of our finest moments, but at least we still had a roof over our heads.

What we wouldn't have for much longer, however, was a car. After we ran out of cash, it basically came down to car or food, so I stopped making payments on the BMW. I tried to buy as much time as I could, but after a while the amount I owed added up to so much that I finally just gave them my new address and told them to come pick it up.

Ah, my second repo. I was on a roll.

But it wasn't over yet. Remember those guys who grilled me in that deposition about covering for Edgar and hiding money? Yeah, well, now that Edgar was MIA, they were coming after me. And not just me. They were coming after Driven. They were suing us for around a million bucks, or some ridiculous amount.

They accused us of fraud, hiding money for Edgar, and a bunch of other stuff we had nothing to do with. The problem was, even though we were 100 percent innocent, we didn't have the money it would have cost to hire a lawyer to fight them, so we decided to settle. We were able to pay them a certain amount a month to get them off our backs for the time being.

But the best was yet to come.

Remember Rodrigo? The nice, sweet, gentle, Spanish recording engineer? Well, he hit me with a lawsuit too. He claimed he was owed tens of thousands of dollars that Edgar had never paid him for engineering services.

I swear, it was like the minute Edgar disappeared, everybody grabbed their flaming torches and started marching in my direction, screaming, "Get the rock star!"

I could kind of understand all the other lawsuits, but this one hurt. I thought Rodrigo was my friend, and the fact that he would turn on me so quickly was a bitter pill to swallow. Edgar had burned all of us financially. I had lost the most money, probably more than anyone else, but that didn't stop Rodrigo from coming after me full force.

We knew we couldn't afford to go to court, so Gary and I decided to sit down with Rodrigo and his attorney to see if we could work out a fair settlement. It was the first time I'd seen Rodrigo in months.

" 'Ello Brian. How are you?" he said, smiling as though nothing had ever happened.

Is this guy kidding me?

"How do you think I'm doing? I'm getting ransacked from every direction, and now you, who I once called a friend, are trying to hang me out to dry like all the others!"

That's what I wanted to say.

What I actually said was, "Hey, Rodrigo. I'm doing okay. How are you?"

The pleasantries out of the way, we all sat down and the discussions began.

"Rodrigo, do you have any idea how much Edgar bled every one of us dry?" I asked. "I put hundreds of thousands of dollars into all our companies, and now I've got nothing, and I've been left here holding the bag. I never had any arrangements with you. You and Edgar always discussed your business on your own. I was never invited into any of those meetings." Then I just let it all out. "You know I'm a single dad with a young daughter. Why are you, my friend, coming after me with another lawsuit?"

If I expected sympathy, I was about to be disappointed.

"Brian," Rodrigo stated matter-of-factly, "I did a lot of work on your album. I was promised payment from Edgar, and I have invoices that have not been paid. My studio is suffering, and I need to be compensated for my work. You have started Driven Music Group, and I think I deserve to get paid from the money you are making through that deal. This is nothing personal, but I have to look out for myself." And with that, he was done talking.

Hmmm. Well, that makes me even angrier because it makes sense.

We tried to reach a settlement, but my idea of fair and Rodrigo's were miles apart. He wanted payment in full, and I wanted him to chill out and accept a smaller, more manageable amount, something I could actually afford.

"Rodrigo," I said, trying to control my anger, "every single person involved with Edgar lost money. Why should you get full payment while everyone else settles for less or nothing?"

But Rodrigo wouldn't budge, so we left.

"You can go ahead and sue us," we said on our way out the door. "There are ten other people ahead of you, so good luck ever seeing a dime."

Jesus, please help me turn the other cheek because I feel like these dudes already smacked one side of my face hard! Oh yeah, and help me forgive because right now I want to rip Rodrigo's polite little head off. Amen.

If Rodrigo would have made even the slightest effort to work with us, I would have found a way to start making payments to him ASAP. Unfortunately for him, he wasn't willing, and I was pretty sure he would end up regretting that decision later.

———

Even though I was being financially torn to shreds, I kept marching on like a soldier and tried to stay positive.

The release date for the album was approaching fast, and since I didn't have a touring band put together yet, we decided to go on a multi-state CD signing tour. With everything else that was happening, I figured it would probably be best if Jennea stayed home, so I arranged for her to stay with a friend. I lucked out big time with that kid. Despite all the chaos in our lives—the move, the repos, the small-change scavenger hunt—she stayed positive. I have no doubt those butterflies she felt in the car that day were God's peace and love and strength because she seemed to radiate those qualities.

Fortunately a little of that peace and love spilled over into the CD tour. We went from Washington to Texas to New York, and many states in between. A lot of fans came out, which felt great too. While we were in Dallas, I met with I Am Second, an online organization that puts together video testimonies of people whose lives have been transformed by Christ. They had invited me to film my story, and I couldn't have been more honored, especially considering that they were trying to get Bono and some other people I respected involved at the time.

Everything on the release tour was going great until I got ready to travel back to Dallas. Then, right before I got on my flight, I got the most grotesque feeling inside for what seemed like no reason whatsoever. I suddenly felt a hatred for everything around me, and I boiled over with that old familiar rage, ready to snap at anyone. In fact, I ended up getting into it with some pretty rude TSA agents at the airport. Thankfully, for the most part I was able to power through it. But I'm telling you, something didn't want me to film that I Am Second video. I was still massively on edge the day of the filming, and the end result definitely carries the seriousness of what I was feeling that day.

All in all, though, the tour was a success, and *Save Me from Myself* shipped over seventy-eight hundred copies in its opening week. It debuted at number twenty-seven in New Zealand, number sixty-three on the Billboard 200, number seven on Billboard's Independent Albums chart, and number three on the Christian Albums chart. Not bad for a solo debut, but it was night and day compared to KoRn sales.

After the album released, Carl and Gary started pushing me to start touring again. Our launch was solid, but it didn't exactly blow the doors off the joint, and they wanted to keep the momentum going. I had been resisting in part because of the vocal problems I'd had in the studio, but more important, because I didn't want to leave Jennea behind for long stretches at a time. I felt like I was caught between a rock and a hard place. On the one hand, more than anything, I wanted to be a good dad—and that meant staying home. But I also needed to make sure Jennea *had* a home. With all my financial problems, if I didn't get my solo career off the ground soon, I couldn't even guarantee that. And if my years in the music business have taught me nothing else, it's that touring moves albums. I couldn't see any other alternative. I decided to go for it.

On the plus side, although I hated to admit it, Jennea *was* getting older, and like most kids her age, she was starting to become more independent—spending time with friends, going to sleepovers—you know, typical tween-age stuff. When I first left KoRn, she clung to me like Velcro. Now she almost seemed to prefer spending time at her friends' houses. It still wasn't an ideal situation, but it did make the prospect of me having to be away for a week or two at a time a little easier.

It was a relief to have the touring decision made, but I still needed a band. To save time and to avoid having to travel any sooner than necessary, we decided to hold open Internet auditions on YouTube with the potential winners flying out to Arizona for a final jam session.

It turned out Ralph, the engineer who mixed my album, was also a mean guitarist, so he was the first guy I chose after he offered to help. The coolest thing about that was he also took over a lot of the leadership responsibilities, which took some of the load off me. And he took a major pay cut to do it, for which I was really grateful.

The other guitar player who tried out passed on our offer and joined Marilyn Manson instead, so we welcomed Scott Von Heldt, who ended up being even better. We also chose Michael Valentine on bass, Dan Johnson on drums, and Brian Ruedy on keyboards.

And with that I officially had my band.

Now it was time to hit the road and test out my vocals at some live shows. After all the craziness I'd been through over the past year and a half, things were finally starting to go my way.

Or so I thought.

CHAPTER 5

IT'S A DOG-EAT-DOG WORLD

The one saving grace amid all the chaos of losing the house, the cars, the businesses, and the friendships was Jennea. That kid was solid as a rock. She never stressed out, wondering, *How is my dad gonna take care of me?* She just played, had fun, and didn't ever think about what could go wrong. She had the kind of blind trust and confidence that I wanted to have in God. Adults can learn a lot from kids. I know mine sure taught me a lot during that uncertain time. That's why I decided to do something extra special for her. I'd been thinking about it a lot, and even though the timing was terrible, I just couldn't resist. So one day while we were driving home from church, I sprang it on her.

"Jennea," I started, bracing for the hysteria, "I don't want you to freak out, and I'm not saying it's for sure, but I was thinking about possibly getting a puppy."

It's a good thing I had a tight grip on the wheel because she screamed so loud I'm surprised it didn't shatter the windshield.

"Oh, Dad, can we? Please can we get a puppy? Please?" she begged.

Oh, man. Now I've done it.

"I'm just thinking about it," I stated very calmly. "If I did . . . would you promise to clean up after it, feed it, and take care of all the other responsibilities that come with a dog?"

"Yes!" she blurted out. "I promise! I pinky swear!"

For those of you who don't have kids, let me tell you, that pinky-swear thing is a pretty big deal. Even though I'd already gotten stuck taking care of the hamster and both guinea pigs, there was no way I was going to be able to say no at this point, and Jennea knew it. As soon as I said I was thinking about it, it was all over.

After several weeks of looking, we finally decided on a Shih Tzu.

We named her Queen after one of Jennea's favorite stuffed animals.

And did that name fit. From the second we brought her home, that puppy acted like royalty and took complete control of the house and our lives.

Here's some free advice: If you ever want a puppy that potty trains quickly, do not get a Shih Tzu. They are the worst! I tried to potty train that thing for months. We bought those potty pads for her, and she went on them some of the time, but if we weren't watching her, she'd go on the carpet in a second.

It was ridiculous.

Even more disturbing, though, was Queen's disgusting habit of eating her own poop when she was a puppy. Sick! I hate to think of how many times she licked our faces before we realized it.

Anyway, we had Queen for more than six months, and as much as Jennea loved the dog, like any eleven-year-old, she also wanted to spend time with her friends. So guess who got stuck at home entertaining the yelping, peeing, poop-eating dog?

Exactly.

Even after a pinky swear.

Then one day, as I was chillin' at home on the couch, Queen

walked in, sniffed the carpet, got in position, and dropped a colossal dump—while staring at me.

I immediately took her to a local vet who had a kennel service on site. As soon as I walked in, I said, "Can you guys please take this dog? Because I'm gonna lose my mind."

The vet who worked there was a nice Spanish gentleman. In fact, he reminded me of Rodrigo.

"Oh my gosh," he said, coming over to scratch Queen's head. "Look at this beautiful, beautiful doggie! What's the little cutie's name?"

"Queen. Do you want her?" I responded only half jokingly.

"Are you serious?" he asked.

"Yeah." I'd had it at that point.

"Let me ask my wife," he said, reaching for his phone.

A few minutes later his wife agreed to take Queen.

Oh man, I thought. *How am I gonna break this to Jennea? She's gonna flip out.*

That afternoon after Jennea got home from school, I sat her down and explained the situation to her.

"Nea," I said calmly, hoping to avoid a huge scene. "Queen living with us isn't working out. We've had her for months, and she still isn't potty trained. I just can't take it anymore. You're growing up fast and you're spending more and more time at your friends' houses, and I get stuck with Queen all day and on weekends too. It's not fair to Queen or to me."

"I'll stay home more, Dad. I promise." Tears started to well up in her eyes, but I stayed focused. I was tired of dealing with Queen's crap—literally.

"No, Nea. I'm sorry. But there is some good news," I said, hoping to bring the situation back under control. "We can still take Queen home once in a while for visits. The vet who's gonna take care of her from now on said we could. He's giving us visiting rights."

"Are you sure?"

"Yeah. That way you can hang out with your friends and still have a dog—part time." I waited for that to sink in. Jennea stared down at her feet for a few seconds, then looked up at me and sheepishly agreed.

To the vet's credit, he stood by his word and gave Jennea full visitation rights with Queen. He would even bring her in to work with him so we could pick her up and take her home for the afternoon or overnight. This part-time puppy-ownership deal—I'd never even heard of it before this—I highly recommend it.

—

After Queen was gone and I was once again king of my own castle, Gary, Carl, and I decided it was time for my new band to do a little bit of touring. Much like everything else in my life, touring proved to be a never-ending series of extreme highs followed by extreme lows. One show would be killer, and the next would be so bad I'd almost want to quit.

For example, our first show was at a big church's mini amphitheater, and not only did we have a lot of time to rehearse in the actual space, but the guy who booked it for us had a connection with someone named Mitch, who owned a helicopter, and he agreed to fly a couple of us to the concert in it. Mitch was so cool that before the concert he flew us through the beautiful desert mountains outside of Scottsdale, Arizona, and afterward went in for a landing right next to the theater where all the fans were waiting in line. Talk about a first-class entrance. And it was a great crowd. The place was packed. Pretty awesome for a solo gig. I was nervous about my voice, and it did start off a little shaky, but I got through it and people didn't really seem to notice. At least I don't think they did. The fans seemed to love it, so I was happy.

Our second show, however, was completely horrible. I could tell it was going to be a bad night when the second I walked into the venue a guy offered me drugs. The show was at a bar, and by the time we took the stage, there were all of about thirty people there. My vocals were good in some spots and bad in others. It was really humbling. Thirty half-interested people standing around a stupid bar watching us play our hearts out while some drunks played pool in the background was definitely a far cry from the KoRn days.

On the upside, though, something else happened that night that was a million miles away from the old days. After the concert, we took a girl to the back of our tour bus to pray for her. She had cancer, and after the show she came up and asked us to pray that she would be healed. That was cool. The back lounge of tour buses were known for many things back in the day, but I can assure you, praying was not one of them.

The extremes of these first two shows became pretty much the norm for the tour. Then one night I hit a point so low I actually quit.

We were in Modesto, California, playing in a little bar, and as soon as I took the stage, I felt that familiar rage welling back up. I think it was just the built-up frustration of performing in so many beaten-down bars with only a few people in attendance every night. Plus, I ran into an old friend earlier at sound check, and I could tell he was on meth. I could feel the rage boiling beneath the surface. It didn't help that I was having all kinds of problems with my mic stand too. It kept falling down over and over again. Then I thought I heard a weird sound on my guitarist Scott's amp, so right in the middle of our live show, I decided to crawl in front of him to turn off his guitar pedal.

I fumed, crawling over wires on my way back to the broken mic stand.

That's when it happened. Right in the middle of singing "Washed by Blood," a song about my redemption, I flipped out and chucked my microphone, almost hitting my drummer in the head. I stormed off the stage without saying a word to the crowd or my band, demanded a driver, left the show, and canceled the rest of the tour. As the car pulled away from the club, guess what came on the radio?

Yep, KoRn. It felt like someone was messing with my life. If someone would've offered me drugs at that moment, I may have actually taken them. I couldn't understand why I continued to struggle year after year with this monster of rage that lived inside of me. It felt evil—like I was encountering demons. And I'm sure I was. Looking back, I think it all stemmed from insecurity, but at the time all I knew was that I hated that strong feeling of anger and rage inside me.

As it happens, the very next night I ended up at a Chris Daughtry (*American Idol*) concert in San Francisco. A pastor friend of mine named Michael Guido was touring with Daughtry, and when I told him about my blowup the night before, he invited me to come out to the show to see if we could work through some of my emotions. It helped a little. But as I watched Daughtry perform, I realized he had everything I wished I had—a great voice, first-class equipment, and a packed crowd. Guido tried his best to talk me off the ledge. I really appreciated it, and I loved hanging with him and Daughtry, but I was also a little resistant to his help. I needed to talk to someone who could really understand what I was going through. So that night I texted my old friend and bandmate Fieldy.

Fieldy had contacted me about a month earlier and asked if I'd be interested in working on a benefit song for our friend Chi from the band Deftones, who was in a coma after getting into a horrible car accident. There were a lot of musicians from other big rock bands involved as well, and I considered Chi a dear old friend, so of course I quickly agreed. After that initial connection, Fieldy and I texted back and forth a few times just to stay connected. He had become a Christian shortly after I had, so between that, our KoRn background, and growing up together we had a lot in common.

We agreed to meet at his house the next day to talk about my meltdown. Man, it felt good to see him again as I walked into his house and gave him a big hug.

"So, are you doing better today?" Fieldy asked.

"I guess," I answered, though I wasn't all that convinced. "I'm not as mental as I was yesterday, but I still can't figure out what God wants from me, man. It's like I have this depression that comes bubbling up out of nowhere, and I can't control it. I've done everything I can think of to get rid of all the residue from my past, but I can't seem to shake the depression, anger, and rage thing."

"Maybe it's no coincidence that you're here right now," he said. "Maybe you're meant to come back to KoRn. As far as I'm concerned, the door is always open."

I thought about that for a second. I also thought about hearing that KoRn song after I stormed offstage. Could that have been a sign? "I don't know, man. I've been going my own way for so long. I'm a completely different person now. Why would I want to play a bunch of songs that I can't relate to anymore?"

"Well, you were angry and aggressive during your meltdown, and KoRn's lyrics are pretty angry and aggressive," he joked.

He had me there. "Yeah, you're right." I laughed.

"Listen, why don't I talk to Jonathan and Munky and see where their heads are at," he suggested. "And if it's not God's will, then the door will slam shut. But if it is . . ."

I have to admit, it sounded good. Over the years the KoRn managers had asked me to come back a few times, but I had ignored them. Sitting at Fieldy's house that morning, though, had me wondering if rejoining KoRn was actually meant to be.

"Yeah," I said. I had nothing to lose. "Go ahead and talk to them, and let's see what happens."

So the next day Fieldy called Munky and Jonathan and asked them what they thought about me coming back to the band, and we got our answer.

They didn't think it was a good idea. They said the timing wasn't ideal since they were already working on a new album.

I was fine with that until about a week later when Munky did an interview saying that I was basically begging them to let me come back. Naturally it went viral, and soon everyone in the rock world started believing the lie. That was the final nail in the coffin. I vowed right then and there never to entertain the idea of going back to KoRn again. Never. Ever. And I was serious about it. So serious that when I wrote my devotional book called *Stronger* in 2009, I dedicated one of the devotionals to the subject and story of never, ever, ever going back to KoRn. (Sounds like a Taylor Swift song.)

On the flip side, more uplifting things were going on in my life at that time—like hanging around with Sonny Sandoval from P.O.D. and his friend Ryan Ries. They were in the process of starting a movement called the Whosoevers, and they asked me to come on board with them. Inspired by Jesus' words in John 3:16, "For God so loved the world that he gave his one and only Son, that whosoever believes in him shall not perish but have eternal life," the Whosoevers started hosting a few huge outreach music festivals where all kinds of different musicians, bikers, and skaters performed and/or shared their testimonies. I had already agreed to speak and perform at their first concert in Las Vegas before my Modesto meltdown, so while I wasn't too excited about getting up in front of a live audience again, I had made a commitment, and I didn't want to disappoint them.

It ended up being exactly what I needed.

There were around fifteen thousand people there, my band performed well, a lot of people shared some absolutely phenomenal stories, and a bunch of people ended up deciding to start a relationship with Jesus. It was inspiring. It was also a perfect reminder that I needed to keep moving forward with my solo career.

In fact, the experience was so good that I decided to resume playing shows and touring with my band once in a while. Most of the shows from then on were one-night in-and-outers or weekend festivals, so I was able to spend a lot of time at home with Jennea, which worked out perfectly.

Over the course of the next year or so, we played around thirty to fifty shows that were totally amazing, and we saw loads of people come to the Lord. Of course, we also played about twenty shows that were a complete joke, but the good ones more than made up for the bad ones.

Some nights I'd tell my story from the stage, and practically the entire crowd would shout a loud prayer with me (with our metal voices) to ask Jesus into their lives. Other nights I'd talk to individual people after the show. One night after our show, we were invited to a fan's house to love on a drug addict who'd been in a bunch of accidents and was in horrible, declining health. Afterward we took a photo with him. When we looked to see how it turned out, we could see a single beam of light shining down only on him in the photo. It was definitely a sign. Another night when we played the Parachute Music Festival in New Zealand, I got to meet a young Make-A-Wish kid and his family. I brought him onstage with me while I spoke to tens of thousands of people and introduced him to the crowd, telling them that we could all learn from the kid (and his family) about staying strong as we face difficulties in life. He passed away about a week later, and I felt truly honored that God would allow me to be a part of something so special during the last few days of his young life. These types of experiences happened again and again. They blew my mind every time.

Broken mic stands, my meltdown, Munky's interview—none of it mattered in the end. All I cared about was seeing people's lives touched. Period. And the whole thing couldn't have come at a better time because back at Driven things were starting to fall apart.

Carl had signed some other artists, but we didn't have enough money to release their albums properly. My solo album was selling okay, but it wasn't enough. We needed some fast cash to stay in business. The problem was we all had horrible credit, so the banks wouldn't touch us.

Then Gary had an idea. He had a couple of friends who were doctors, so we decided to approach them for a loan. It took some convincing, but they eventually agreed to give us a loan for about $200,000, but only if we each agreed to sign a guarantee separately. So, in what was one of the worst decisions I'd ever made as a businessman and as a father, I agreed that if Driven couldn't pay back the doctors' loan, I would sign over all my KoRn royalties. Yeah. Just let that sink in for a minute.

Gary and Carl signed their lives away, too, but at the end of the day, my KoRn royalties were the only real collateral worth a substantial amount. After we got the money from them, we were even more motivated to make the label a success. We had a lot of ideas, and we worked really hard over the next few months to release new albums and build our company.

As the months passed, we tried to stretch the doctors' loan as far as we could. The problem was that Gary, Carl, and I were each a financial mess individually, so we were forced to use some of the loan to cover our personal living expenses. The majority of the loan went into the company, but we still weren't making enough to pay the doctors back in a timely fashion.

To their credit, the doctors were very patient and gave us multiple chances to catch up. Still, poor Gary was stressing every single day because these guys were his close friends. It was a bad situation, and it was only getting worse.

Around that time Driven was talking about putting out my second solo record, working with a producer named Rob Graves in Nashville, Tennessee, who I sought out. Rob had produced the Grammy-nominated band Red, who I was a fan of, so I flew out to

Nashville to work with him for a few days. All of us at Driven thought releasing another album was not only the next natural step for my career, but it might solve our money problems as well.

While I was there, I talked to Rob about some of the problems I was having. I actually was starting to wonder if I should find someone else to manage me. Gary was a friend, but my solo career wasn't exactly skyrocketing, and now my KoRn royalties were on the line. I started to sense that things were not totally adding up at Driven. I was trusting Gary and Carl just like before, but by this point I was involved enough to start having some concerns. Something had to change. Although the thought of cutting ties with friends left me feeling uncomfortable and stressed out, I was starting to believe it was meant to be. So Rob set up a meeting between me and David Williams from Union Entertainment Group, Red's management company at the time.

When I walked into Union Entertainment to meet with David, the first thing out of my mouth the minute we sat down was, "If you are taking this meeting because you think I might get back with KoRn, then we should stop right now. That's *never* going to happen."

David replied, "That's not why we took this meeting. I saw your I Am Second video. I don't really care about KoRn. Don't get me wrong, it will always be part of your story—a hugely important part of your past—but we are interested in your future and where we think you can go."

We talked a little longer, and after hearing some of Union's ideas about my future recording career, I decided to sign with them a couple of days later.

Even though I had new management in place, all of us moved forward with my relationship with Driven intact. I was one of the owners after all, so the plan was still to make record two and release it through Driven. Gary and Carl were still very involved with David and the team at UEG. I even had several discussions with David about keeping Gary on as my tour manager.

It was during these first couple of months that David set me up with a new attorney named Lannie Cates and a business manager and CPA named Jamie Humphres. This was the first time I was surrounded with a full team since I'd left KoRn. David and Jamie immediately started digging into everything—even some of the unresolved royalty issues with KoRn. Gary sent David and my new attorney all my contracts and royalty statements from everything I had been doing since KoRn. He also received a nice box full of law-suits left over from all the mess of the Edgar days. David, Lannie, and Jamie eventually reviewed all my paperwork and even started getting into the books and records from Driven.

It didn't take that long before David called me in for a meeting.

"Brian, you seriously have a real mess here." Then he sat back in his chair and very matter-of-factly said, "If I were you, I would cut all ties with these guys."

"But we are tied together in so many ways," I countered. "And even though everything's kind of a mess right now, we've been through a lot together. Besides," I added, "we're all friends."

He shook his head. "Friends or not, Brian, you really should think about keeping your distance from both of them. It would benefit you and your future career best to clean up this mess. My recommenda-tion is to cut ties with these guys and start fresh."

"You don't understand though," I explained. "A lot of those deci-sions were my idea."

I felt so bad at the thought of dumping them out of my life, so I kept trying. "What about tour managing?" I asked. "I should at least let Gary tour manage for me or something, so he can be a part of things in some way. I don't want to just disappear on him."

David wouldn't budge. "Brian, I know it may be hard, but there is no way it would be beneficial for you. Trust me," he added. "Managers are not supposed to bring risky deals to their artists and allow them to sign contracts that could very well bring financial ruin to them.

Managers are supposed to look out for their artists and protect them against things like that. This is gonna get messy no matter what."

As hard as it was to hear, I knew he was right. But I was torn. Part of me wanted to tell David to get lost because I barely knew the guy, but he had already set me up with a great team and had a clear plan to help lead me to success, so even though it was difficult, I followed all his advice.

Now it was time to face the music with Gary and Carl. I decided to start with Gary, so I wrote him an e-mail.

Gary,

While I was in Nashville, I met with some guys from Union Entertainment Group. It's nothing personal, but things just aren't working out with all of us at Driven. I have to think about Jennea, man. Union has some really good ideas about how to get my solo career going so I can gain some income for me and Jennea. So, I decided to sign with them. They're advising me to cut ties with you guys. I tried to find a way to keep you on board somehow, but after talking to them and to their lawyer, there's just no way to make it work.

Gary replied right back totally disagreeing with everything David said, of course. I had known him for years, and I could tell he was really upset.

Man, one of the worst things in life for me is having to deal with confrontation and drama. I knew this was going to be hard, and Gary's reaction didn't make it any easier. Still, I had to stick to my guns. It was my financial future at stake. This wasn't just about me. I had a kid to think about.

I'm sorry, man. I feel terrible, but I gotta take their advice. You, Carl, and I gave this our best shot, and it didn't turn out as we had hoped. I have to move on for me and my daughter's sake. I'm really sorry.

Later that afternoon, Gary spoke with Carl, and then he told the doctors about my decision. Needless to say, none of them were happy. I'm sure they were all nervous, but it was the best decision for me. Despite David's concerns, however, I was still open to putting my second solo album out through Driven. It wasn't much, but at that point it was the least I could offer Gary and Carl.

Meanwhile, I continued to fly back and forth between Phoenix and Nashville to meet with Union and their attorney, and during one of the visits, I was invited to make a guest appearance onstage with Red at the Dove Awards—an awards show that primarily celebrated soft, mainstream Christian artists. As a heavy rock band, Red didn't really fit in, but I thought it was great that they included them. If nothing else, at least it helped broaden the acceptance of different genres in Christian music.

Still, when Red hit the stage, you could see the uneasiness on many of the audience's faces. It was hilarious! I came onstage to join Red after their intro, and as I walked out my guitar strap broke, so I had to play the rest of the song holding my guitar up with a couple of fingers while strumming the guitar strings at the same time. It was crazy, but kind of raw and cool, so we all had a good laugh about it afterward. As for the crowd, they didn't know what to do with us. Most of the audience were conservative Christians, and we were really, really loud, which freaked them out. I think the only one in the audience who got us was the artist Toby Mac; he was actually standing up and rocking out. Regardless, it was a great experience.

After the show I met a guy named Greg McCollum, whose wife, Angie, worked with I Am Second, the organization I'd filmed my testimony for. I mentioned that I was thinking about relocating to Nashville to be closer to my new management team, and about a week later I received an e-mail from Angie offering to show Jennea and me around the city the next time we were in town.

I have to admit, the thought of getting out of Arizona and starting over sounded great. So on my next Nashville trip, I decided to take Angie up on her offer and brought Jennea with me to check the city out.

I didn't want to mess up Jennea's life by uprooting her and making her start all over again, but I figured it couldn't hurt to go and see.

Okay, God, if moving to Nashville is the right thing for us to do, just show us a sign.

When we were driving around in our rental car on our first day in Nashville, Jennea looked at me and said something shocking.

"Dad, I don't know why I'm saying this, but I think we should move here."

It was crazy. This kid was just turning twelve. There was no natural reason she should've been so open to leaving her hometown. Looks like I got my sign.

"Well, if we did decide to move," I said, "it'd be great timing because you're entering seventh grade this year and all your friends are going to different junior high schools anyway."

She thought about that for a second and then said, "Yeah, that's true."

After touring the city with Angie for a few days, Jennea and I were officially sold—we were moving to Nashville.

"So are you excited to start fresh in a different state, Nea?" I asked on the flight home.

"Yeah, I think I'll like it," she said. "It's pretty there, and the people are nice."

"I know it's a big change for us. Are you sure you're okay with it?" And once again, Jennea showed the same unwavering trust she had shown all year.

"Yeah. It just feels like we're supposed to go there," she replied, sounding wise beyond her years. "Besides, I can still see my old friends on Facebook and stuff."

"Totally," I said, still happily oblivious to the destructive problems from teens spending too much time on social media.

———

Before we could move, there were two final orders of business to take care of—my band's second big festival show and first overseas tour in Europe. I arranged for Jennea to stay with my parents out in Bakersfield while I was in Europe. She loved visiting them because she had a bunch of cousins who lived there too. They would all hang out and find fun things to do and even visit my parents' beach condo two hours away in Pismo Beach. I figured she'd have so much fun that she'd barely even notice I was gone.

Before we headed out to Europe, we were scheduled to play our first festival show since David started managing us, and it was nothing less than comical. David flew out with me to Texas, and we were hanging out in the hotel lobby right after we arrived when we got word that the entire festival got canceled because of weather—on the day of the event. Unbelievable.

That day was also the first meeting David took with the band. Basically David handed them Profit and Loss Statements and had to tell them that the financial numbers Driven had told them to expect were pretty unrealistic. (To their credit, Driven didn't know what to expect financially for my project because I hadn't toured much.) This was the beginning of the end for a couple of the band members because a normal person couldn't survive easily on what David said they would make.

This was also when we all had a discussion about adding a couple of KoRn songs to our set. I was really resistant at first, but the more we talked, I ended up considering our song "Blind," mainly because the song was in my vocal range, and I could sing it easily. We talked about how my fans needed to hear something familiar to ease into the new solo stuff, especially since Europe was right around the corner.

The band was stoked about traveling to Europe. David had booked us to play cities in Germany, Sweden, Denmark, the Faroe Islands, Ukraine, and about a half dozen other countries. It all sounded exciting, but none of us had any clue what we were in for. We had to fly almost every day, lugging all our gear with us; Ruedy, our keyboardist, had so much gear that he was constantly exploding on everyone, and we couldn't blame him, handling all the weight he had to carry.

On top of that, it seemed like everywhere we went something weird happened. It was almost like we were living out the movie *This Is Spinal Tap*. I somehow managed to fall on my butt three times during one show because I kept tripping over wires and speakers. And unbeknownst to me, one of the band members brought a really expensive camera along with him and started taking all these pictures of young girls at the airports when they weren't looking. One day a mom caught him and started screaming at him, and the next thing you know, a couple of guys came over and started threatening him. At least I think they were threatening him; it was hard to tell since none of us spoke the language. But they were definitely not happy.

Then when we got to Amsterdam, one of the guys started hanging out in smoke shops, getting drunk—he'd opted out of the legal weed. He drank a lot on that tour, and it really got to me because he was an annoying drunk, always slurring his words and smelling like a hobo.

In Poland we discovered that one of our promoters had lied and didn't book us homebound connecting flights, so we had to hire a car service to drive us from Poland to Ukraine. Instead of a simple two-hour flight, we ended up taking a cramped, miserable twelve-hour car ride with two drivers who didn't speak a word of English. Oh, and while we were driving across the border into Ukraine at five o'clock in the morning, we actually passed a dead body on the freeway—a casualty from a motorcycle accident. My heart sunk.

Next, Ralph, my buddy who helped me get the band started, decided to quit right toward the end of the tour.

"Dude, I don't know how much longer I can do this. You know I have my studio at home with countless bands wanting me to produce them. I love you, man, and I don't want to leave you hanging, but I don't think I can stick around after this tour."

"I understand," I told him. "Just do what you gotta do." I couldn't blame him. I was about ready to walk at that point myself. In fact, I already tried to quit.

Finally, for a cherry on top, my parents forgot my birthday. Hilarious! When I didn't hear from them, I decided to give them a call, and they had no idea. It actually ended up being pretty funny.

"So, is anything special going on today?" I asked.

"No, just hanging around the house," my dad answered.

Seriously?

"Nothing about this day is special?" I asked again.

"No, why?"

Unbelievable.

I gave them one last chance. "So, you're saying nothing is special about today at all?"

Silence. Then . . .

"Oh my gosh, Brian! Happy birthday! We're so sorry. Happy birthday, son!"

I just laughed. "It's okay. I've forgotten your birthdays before. Now we're even."

When all was said and done, nobody made a dime on that tour. In fact we didn't even make enough money to cover all our costs.

It wasn't all bad though. Some of the shows were really big festivals, so we got to play in front of tons of people a few times. But perhaps the coolest thing that happened on the road was getting this e-mail from Angie:

Brian,

I found a house for you today!! It is an older home that sits on two acres. It has three bedrooms and two baths, downstairs and upstairs. The home is clean, and with a little paint (they said you could paint) it would look fabulous!! It has a great sitting area in the back; you look off into acreage and the woods. The upstairs is perfect to set up a studio or music room.

I love it, but I love old houses. I like their charm and character.

I can go take pictures if you would like. It will go fast, so we need to work quickly if you are interested.

Angie

She even shot some video of the house and e-mailed it to me. It was perfect! I was so excited that I quickly e-mailed the landlord from Germany. My credit was horrible, but I had enough money left from my last royalty check to pay six months' rent in advance, so he e-mailed me back the lease, and I signed it before we even left Europe. And just like that, Jennea and I were ready to move to Nashvegas.

As soon as I got back to Arizona, I quietly yet quickly started to figure out how to move out of town ASAP. I knew all my creditors weren't going to magically disappear, but to some extent I still wanted to go where nobody could find me for a while. I needed a little time to get a plan together for how and when I was going to be able to pay everyone back.

I decided to hire my drummer, Dan, to drive all our belongings from Arizona to Nashville in a U-Haul. So we packed up everything from our two-bedroom apartment along with everything we'd put in storage after losing the house. I even had him tow my car on a trailer. We gave Dan a two-day head start and then flew to Nashville to meet him.

You'd think that moving from Phoenix to Nashville would be an improvement when it comes to hot weather, but no. The day we moved into our new house ended up being the hottest day of the year. Literally. It was a record breaker. And the humidity was ridiculous. It made the heat seem a lot worse than it ever felt in Phoenix. And let me tell you, there's nothing like lugging bed frames, mattresses, box springs, tables, dressers, mirrors, about two dozen boxes of clothes, books, and other heavy things up a full flight of stairs in 105-degree heat and 99 percent humidity.

Within a few days, though, Jennea and I started to settle in.

"So, Jennea, what do you think of the place?" I asked over a dinner of mac and cheese in our new kitchen.

"I like it, but it's hot here," she said. "Like Phoenix, but worse."

I had to laugh. Was this my kid or what? "I know." I smiled. "But hey, we are gonna have a great new life in Nashville. God definitely wants us here. Just watch what he does."

While settling into our new way of life in Nashville, my new manager, David, was trying to help me untangle the financial mess I had left behind in Phoenix. My new lawyer, Lannie, helped me prioritize the issues that needed the most—and quickest—attention. Item number one was Rodrigo. I decided to offer him a settlement again in hopes of making the whole situation go away once and for all. I wasn't in the mood for a big emotional confrontation, so I sent him an e-mail.

Rodrigo,

I just want to put all this behind us. Let's try and work out a deal, man. You think I owe you all this money, and I think Edgar owes it to you. But I think I can get my hands on a few thousand dollars in the near future from royalties. What if I pay you $20–$30K?

He e-mailed me back the next day and said he needed to discuss it all with his lawyer.

Lord, let him at least be open to working with me on this.

Two days later, I heard back: no deal.
I was completely dumbfounded.

Jesus . . . Rodrigo just smacked my other cheek. I have no cheeks left!

Having struck out with Rodrigo, I decided to try to make a different Edgar mess go away. Remember Edgar's old business partners? The guys who dragged me into that deposition? The guys who Gary and I settled with, agreeing to make monthly payments to avoid a costly trial? Even though it was completely ridiculous that they expected me to pay them anything, I ended up giving them a chunk of money to make the monthly payments go away. They didn't give me much of a break by paying in full, but I just wanted them gone, and it cost me a pretty penny. Rodrigo's lawyer would have been wise to accept my settlement because after I paid those guys off I had practically nothing left.

I needed to get to work. Finalizing my second solo album seemed like a good way to generate some income. Despite David's warning, I was still in talks with Gary about putting the album out through Driven. The problem was, Gary and Carl wanted to borrow more money to launch the album, and given my current financial state, I just couldn't do that. We were already in deep with the doctors, and I owed creditors hundreds of thousands more. There was no way I could borrow any more or be involved with the label if they borrowed. Like everything else around us, the label was sinking fast. That was clear to me, but Gary and Carl didn't agree.

Shortly before I had left on my European tour, David started requesting all of Driven's sales and financial records. There were a lot of heated e-mails flying back and forth due to disagreements over how much each partner had taken out of Driven.

Meanwhile, the doctors were fuming, and they decided to come after the three of us with everything they had. The thing is, I never wanted to leave the doctors hanging; I just wanted to work out a way that Gary, Carl, and I could pay them back a third each. I would've had to wait a year or so to start making payments because I was broke, but I had every intention of reimbursing them. The doctors, however, didn't care what my intentions were. They wanted their money back immediately, so they did what I feared the most—they lawyered up, stopped responding to us, and went after my KoRn royalties. To say the entire situation was messy would have been the understatement of the century.

After reviewing all of Driven's financial records, my new management team advised me to hire a lawyer back in Arizona and sue Driven for things that I wasn't sure I agreed with, but I followed their advice anyway. They also advised me to add the doctors to the lawsuit as well. The whole thing made me feel sick to my stomach. I had never sued anybody in my entire life, and now here I was, suing people I had been close friends and business partners with just months earlier. It was absurd.

Yes, Gary and Carl may have made mistakes, and no, they didn't give me very wise counsel on things, but deep down I thought they were both good guys who had helped me a lot over the past two years.

Suing them went against everything in my nature. But things had gotten so bad that I was told there weren't any other options.

To make matters worse, because my unfinished second album was still under contract with Driven (which I was no longer a part of), legally it belonged to the label. They wouldn't let me release any of it unless we all agreed on a settlement, and without a new record I couldn't move forward with my career. The whole thing was a huge catastrophe.

There were a lot of other points of contention, but the long and the short of it was that Gary and Carl disagreed with my new management team, and my management team disagreed with them.

So with no cash flow and Driven holding the release of my second album, there was only one thing left to do. I had to sue my friends. One night I prayed:

Lord, this is completely insane. I realize that I'm supposed to walk through trials, but this is crazy. My management team is advising me to sue Driven. I don't want to sue anyone, but all of us are at complete odds with each other. I gotta ask, Jesus. Where are you in this? I thought after Edgar was gone, everything would even out and start getting better, but now look what's happened. How much can one man be expected to take before he cracks?

I couldn't believe where my life had ended up. It seemed as if every single thing I had tried to do—outside of my relationship with Jesus—had failed miserably.

I had dozens of enemies chasing me. I owed hundreds of thousands of dollars on a foreclosed house, credit cards, the meat delivery vans, the BMW, Rodrigo, Edgar's baggage, lawyers, doctors, you name it. I was buried, and I couldn't see how I was ever going to be able to financially satisfy everyone that was after me.

I had officially hit rock bottom.

It was time to file for bankruptcy.

CHAPTER 11

Confession: I used to think that only complete losers filed for bankruptcy.

How hard is it to manage your money? I would think when I heard of someone falling into financial ruin.

But over the past several years, my eyes have been opened to a lot of things, and I've learned some incredibly valuable lessons—one of which is that financial catastrophes can happen to anyone. It has nothing to do with whether you're a good person or a bad person, how hard you work, or what kind of family you come from. Sometimes we just get beaten down by circumstances beyond our control. Look at me. I came from a great family, had an massively successful music career, and though I was careless with my money after I left KoRn, I was working as hard as I could to provide a stable, happy life for my daughter. Yet there I was—tapped out, desperate, and up to my eyebrows in debt.

I'll admit that I allowed my faith in God to be twisted into unwarranted faith in certain people, which turned me into a complete idiot in many ways. I made a lot of mistakes by being too risky and not playing it safe with my money, and yes, it was very foolish.

It was also very complicated. Over the next few weeks, I met with a couple of different bankruptcy attorneys to talk through my options. And it turns out, there were a lot.

The first guy I met with told me I wasn't eligible for a chapter 13 reorganization because I owed too much money. He said that I could apply for a chapter 7, but that would mean giving up all my future residual income, aka my KoRn royalties, and I definitely didn't want to do that. So I moved on to attorney number two, a guy named Griffin.

When I first met Griffin, I thought he looked too young to be an attorney, but I'll say this for him—the kid knew his stuff. I explained my entire financial situation to him, and after we talked for a while, he came back with a great solution. It's called a chapter 11 reorganization plan.

Normally, a chapter 11 plan is reserved for businesses that owe more than $300,000 (which, by the way, is the cut-off for chapter 13). It allows them to pay back their creditors less than what they actually owe them. It's a little uncommon for individual people to file for chapter 11, but thanks to the ridiculous amount of debt I had racked up, I qualified. *Finally, a break.*

As Griffin started drawing up the paperwork, I felt a strange sense of relief. I was broke, but at least I could see some light at the end of the tunnel. It felt almost like I was getting a fresh start.

I say *almost* because the doctors still wanted a piece of me, and they weren't about to let a little thing like me filing for bankruptcy get in their way.

Don't get me wrong. I always knew the doctors were good guys. I think that when they gave Driven the money, it wasn't so much an investment on their part as it was helping out a good friend. They really liked Gary, and I'm sure they just wanted to see him happy and successful in life like they were. But as soon as they felt like they were getting taken advantage of, they got understandably angry and went on the attack. And I was their target.

I pleaded with them over e-mail to give me a chance to find a way to pay them back, but they didn't want to hear it. They just wanted their money back immediately. Gary and Carl were making a few payments to them, but in the end it was me they really wanted. And because I had signed a personal guarantee, I owed them every last penny. Desperate and out of options, I sent them one last e-mail, begging for mercy to come up with a payment plan, but I got no response.

They weren't going to let up until they saw money in their hands. In fact, one of them even hired a lawyer to contest my bankruptcy and have it thrown out. It was intense. Technically, they were completely justified; I had willingly put my KoRn royalties up as collateral for the loan. But I had Jennea to think about. All I was asking for was to be left with enough money to take care of my kid and to pay the doctors back as quickly as I could with whatever extra money I had after living expenses.

For the moment we were getting by. We didn't have much, but I had enough money to pay Griffin's law firm and all my bills. If the doctors' lawyer got her way, though, I would've been completely wiped out. Thankfully the publishing companies froze my royalties until the court could decide who was entitled to what.

Once the doctors realized this, things got ugly. Their lawyer accused me of fraud. They pointed out that a judge back in Arizona had handed down a judgment against me because I had put my KoRn royalties up as collateral in the initial loan agreement way before I filed for bankruptcy, so I had no right to withhold them now.

Fortunately, Griffin found some obscure Tennessee law that protected me from the Arizona judgment. I didn't understand how it worked then, and I still don't understand it now. But there's one thing I do know for sure—my heavenly Father was watching out for me.

God knew my heart. He knew I wanted—and fully intended—to pay the doctors back. I just needed time and help to do it.

The doctors' lawyer had a different perspective. She was convinced that I had deliberately moved to Nashville with the intent of defrauding them and was dead set on dragging me back into court to prove it.

If they only knew I wasn't smart (or crooked) enough to come up with a plan like that.

Things were beyond rational at this point. I'd already tried reasoning with them, and it didn't work. Now it was time to let my lawyer do the talking and let the whole mess run its course through the legal system. It was "everyone get the rock star" time again, and frankly, I was sick of it. I needed a break.

I didn't get one.

While we were waiting for the court to decide my financial fate, I went out on the road with my band to play some shows. But about ten days into the tour as we landed in Greensboro, North Carolina, I got called back to Nashville to address the fraud charges.

By the time I got back to the airport in Nashville the next night, it was late and I was feeling tired and grumpy. I took the bus to parking lot B where I'd left my car, and as I was pulling out of the lot, I noticed a plain white van driving very slowly off to my left. There were two guys in it, and they were just staring at me. As they drove past me, I got behind them but realized they were going too slow, so I decided to floor it and blow past them on the right. That's when they turned their red and blue lights on. I had just blown past an unmarked airport police van.

You have got to be kidding me!

I quickly pulled over and rolled down my window while the two of them started walking toward my car. And they were ticked.

"What were you thinking trying to pass us like that?" they asked, shining a flashlight in my face. "We had to swerve out of the way because you cut us off!"

That wasn't exactly true. I didn't cut them off. I just passed them—very, very quickly. Still, I wasn't in a position to argue, so I politely responded, "Sorry, officers. I thought you were somebody else, and it seemed like I had plenty of room to get around you."

They glanced at each other, then back at me. They weren't buying it.

"License and registration, please."

I handed my paperwork to the one standing closest to the window, and he started walking back toward the van. But the other one just stood there staring at me. It was starting to get uncomfortable. After a few seconds he followed his partner back to the van.

What is that guy's problem?

A few minutes later the van door opened, and the cop that had been staring at me so intently walked back over to my car, leaned down, handed me my license, and said, "I saw you speak at Cornerstone Christian Festival last summer."

Doh! Busted. Sometimes I forget I don't exactly look like your average, ordinary guy next door. Then his partner appeared in the window.

"Mr. Welch, I want you to know that we could have issued you a reckless driving citation."

Oh, awesome, I thought, my spirits lifting a little. *I'm finally gonna catch a break!*

"But instead I'm giving you a ticket for making an unsafe passing of another motor vehicle," he said, handing the ticket through the window.

Wow. Never a dull moment.

The next day I stood in court feeling like an innocent man accused of a crime he didn't commit.

But I was ready. Remember that suit I wore to the *High School*

Musical 2 premiere? The one that earned me the nickname Gator? Well, guess what I wore to court? Yep, and I was stylin'. But that wasn't all. A few days earlier I had heard an intense online teaching about God being not only our Father but our perfect Judge, and how by faith, and by using our imagination, we can come boldly to his throne in the court of heaven to find help in any situation. After I slipped into my gator suit that morning, I spent a few minutes pleading my case with him.

> *God, you are everything to me. My relationship with you gives me everything my life needs. So right now I come to you in your position as my perfect Judge. I come boldly before your throne in heaven. I choose to believe I am entering into the heavenly courts by faith right now. You know me, and you know I want to make things right with my creditors. I am asking for your help to declare me innocent of these fraud charges. I didn't move to Nashville to defraud anyone. I moved here for music by your leading. I just need more time to pay the doctors and all my other creditors back. Please look at my situation and judge fairly in my favor, so I can make everything right with these people and move on from this. Please, in Jesus' name, give me justice.*

As I stood in the Nashville courthouse that morning, explaining my story to the judge, I had no doubt that the ultimate Judge in heaven's courts had my back, but I was still a little scared.

> *Jesus, I know you know what this feels like. You were innocent and accused of all kinds of junk you didn't do. Be with me, Lord.*

The state judge, on the other hand . . .

"Mr. Welch, let's stick to the facts of the case, please," he stated flatly, cutting me off in the middle of my story. "We need to get through this quicker."

The guy actually sounded annoyed. *My daughter's future is hanging in the balance, and this guy just cut me off!*

Thankfully, my lawyer stepped in and helped me lay out the facts quickly.

"Mr. Welch," he led, "can you please tell the court exactly why you moved to Nashville last year?"

"Yes. I moved to Nashville because I had just hired a new management team that was based here, and I wanted to be closer to them."

I also made it clear that I had no idea there was some random law in Tennessee that would protect me from past rulings in Arizona and that I never had any intention of defrauding anyone.

When I finished pleading my case, I tried to get a read on the judge, but the guy was completely stone-faced.

My attorney sat down, and the doctors' lawyer spent about twenty minutes rehashing my testimony, trying to get me to trip up or catch me in a lie, but there was no chance of that.

It all came down to the judge. Given the way he had cut me off earlier and the emotionless way he listened to my testimony, it wouldn't have surprised me in the least if he had found me guilty.

That's why I was so floored when he announced his verdict.

"I don't see any fraudulent action in Mr. Welch moving his daughter and himself to Tennessee to start over," he stated very matter-of-factly. Then he brought the whole ugly ordeal to a close with the pound of a gavel and two beautiful little words: "Not guilty."

Bam! Yes! That's what I'm talkin' about!

It was a temporary victory. Over the next few weeks, I got called into court a couple more times while the doctors' attorneys battled with me and my lawyer, trying to shake loose every last penny I had. Then, to add insult to injury, the IRS started in and tried to sucker punch me too. Apparently, they weren't happy with the reorganization plan Griffin and I had set up.

I was starting to feel like a dead animal carcass on the side of the road with a pack of buzzards circling overhead, waiting for a chance to swoop down and start picking the meat off my bones.

Please, God. Let this mess come to an end.

Then something unbelievable happened. Apparently, the doctors grew as weary as I was of the whole ordeal, and they finally agreed to a settlement. I would pay them half of every royalty check I received until they were paid back with interest.

See? Was that so hard?

Then things got even better. A few weeks after the doctors called off the dogs, I got an e-mail from Griffin telling me that the judge sided with us and rejected the IRS's attempt to stop the proposed settlement.

Brian,

Congratulations, the plan was confirmed! The battle with the IRS was resolved peacefully, so no issues should be remaining. I bet it feels great that you can finally put the bankruptcy in your rearview mirror. The case can't be closed until a "final decree" is entered, which won't happen until the first payment under the plan is made. We'll get you what's called a "plan payment spreadsheet" that will tell you who needs to be paid and the amount of every check that has to be written. That should make things easier for you.

I've attached the confirmation order that you've seen before (which lays out the settlement terms), but it looks much nicer being signed by a judge. Congratulations again.

Griffin

"Jennea, get in here!" I screamed.

"What?" she said, sounding a little freaked out.

"Read this," I said, turning my laptop in her direction. I had tried to keep the bankruptcy stuff from Jennea as much as I could so she wouldn't stress out, but she had picked up bits and pieces here and there, and she knew I'd been pretty tense the last few months.

"Whoa, awesome!" she said, smiling. "So does this mean you don't have to go into court anymore?"

"Yep. No more court for me!" I was so happy, I almost burst into tears. I could finally start walking into the light at the end of the tunnel. But make no mistake, I was still in the tunnel.

The Driven lawsuit was still in full effect. It may have taken a team of lawyers to deal with the doctors and the IRS, but I genuinely believed that Gary and Carl were different. So I decided to reach out to them myself.

"Listen, Carl, I don't want to spend another five grand on a lawyer to go to court over this," I explained over the phone. "Is there any chance you guys would be willing to try and settle this thing with me out of court?"

It turns out I was right about those guys. They *were* reasonable.

"Sounds good to me," Carl answered, sounding as relieved to be done with the whole ordeal as I was. "Honestly, I wanted this whole thing done with long ago. I'll have my lawyer get in touch with your manager, and we'll work something out, okay?"

"Thanks, man. I really appreciate it." And I did.

The three of us went back and forth a few times on possible terms until we finally reached an agreement we could all live with. And then, just like that, it was over. Rodrigo, the banks from my foreclosed house, and everyone else were all included in my bankruptcy; they had all been awarded a specific amount the court allowed them to get paid under the US chapter 11 bankruptcy code. So once I settled with Driven, that was it. No more lawsuits. No more accusations. No more stress. The only thing left to do was come up with a few hundred thousand dollars to make payments on the rulings the courts had handed down. I had no idea how that was going to happen, but I had come this far, and I knew Jesus would never let me fall on my face this close to the finish line. Now I could turn my attention to new hurdles.

To make up for the fact that I was traveling a lot more, I had started taking Jennea with me on some of our shorter road trips. It was great having her out on the road with me, and she really seemed to enjoy it. There were, however, a couple of drawbacks that I hadn't anticipated. For one thing, she was having trouble making friends at her new school. She had met a few girls that she kind of clicked with, but nothing that sparked any kind of deep friendship. Most of the girls she connected with had family members in the music industry, which meant they spent a lot of time on the road too. That's one of the downsides of life in the music industry. It's sometimes hard to find and maintain solid friendships at home when you're on the road a lot.

It's also hard for the kids to keep up with their schoolwork. Jennea did okay most of the time, but she had a little trouble remembering to write down and follow through with some of her homework responsibilities, which led to missing assignments.

Complicating matters even more was the fact that I only had her in school part time. She had regular classes on Tuesdays and Thursdays, but the rest was all done at home. I had enrolled her in this type of school because I figured it would be easier for her when she had to go out of town with me, but all it seemed to do was mess her up academically and make it harder for her to make new friends. As with the hamster and the puppy fiascos, my intentions were good, but the results? Not so much.

Since seventh grade was proving to be a challenge for Jennea, I decided to hire a nanny for a little while so I could go on a couple of short tours and she could stay at home and focus on her schoolwork. Angie, who helped us find our house, started asking around for me, and we ended up hiring a sweet girl named Anna. Anna happened to be the daughter of legendary Christian recording artist Michael W. Smith. I used to listen to Michael's worship music a little bit back when I first came to Christ, so to have his daughter looking after my daughter was pretty cool. Knowing that Jennea was surrounded by honest, caring people set my mind at ease while I was on the road.

Jennea also got a kick out of it. Michael and his wife, Debbie, were connected to so many people in the entertainment industry that we never knew who was going to stop by the house. One night I called to check in, and even I couldn't believe who was there.

"Oh my gosh, Dad . . . you are never gonna guess who is cooking dinner for us right this second," she said with excitement.

"Who?"

"Guess," Jennea said, barely holding it together.

"Bono?" I asked. I had heard that Bono and Michael were friends.

"No!" she said, full of preteen attitude.

"Then who?" I shot back. "I don't have all night, Nea. I have to play a show."

"Jesus!"

I laughed out loud. "Come on, Jennea. Who is it?"

"Jesus!" she repeated. "It's that guy who played Jesus in *The Passion of the Christ* movie! He's cooking us dinner!"

Whoa! Jim Caviezel was cooking steak for my kid. If that wasn't a sign that God was with us in all our trials, I don't know what is.

We had a few bumps in the road during Jennea's seventh-grade year, but it seemed like God always let cool things like the Jesus dinner fall into our laps at the perfect time.

During that year I ran into someone who used to work for Jennea's favorite band, Blink-182. They were able to get us tickets and backstage passes to a huge festival where Blink was playing. When I surprised Jennea with it while we were at dinner with my bandmates, she didn't believe me. But when she finally realized it was for real, she broke down and cried right at the table. The date for the concert approached very quickly, and the next thing we knew we were walking into the festival gates. Right before Blink went onstage, Jennea got to meet all the band members and take pictures with them. She was blown away.

When it came time for Jennea to start eighth grade, I decided to try online homeschooling full time. David and I had been talking a lot about the possibility of me touring more, and with all the payments I had to make to the doctors, the IRS, and all my other creditors, I wasn't going to be able to afford a nanny much longer. That meant Jennea was going to have to come out on the road with us. So I started checking out online curriculums. I wasn't sure it was the best situation for Jennea, but given our circumstances I really didn't see any other option.

Angie offered to help us out and let Jennea stay with her family while I toured, but Jennea had just turned thirteen and was getting a little testy as well as starting to put up walls around herself to keep people out.

Of course, had Jennea known what was coming just a few months down the road, she might have been a little more receptive to Angie's offer. While she was struggling to finish out seventh grade, my solo band was having a few problems of its own, and the solution was going to take Jennea about as far away from normal home life as you could get.

By the fall of 2011 my band hit a low that made us question if it was wise to continue. We had booked a tour with Decyfer Down, and normally they did pretty well, but our tour with them was a letdown due to promoters not actually promoting the shows. One night after another nearly empty show, I poured out my heart to God in a letter.

God,

I'm sick of touring. I'm sick of being a failure. Why aren't things picking up for us? Why am I so miserable every time we go out on tour? I sometimes feel like I don't even want to do music anymore. I think I'd rather speak to people full time or something. After eight years being gone, I know me and KoRn are over and done with, but why am I failing so much in this solo music mess? For me to continue with all this, I'm gonna need a few changes. I need to start over with my bandmates. We need a new band name. I want a record label to partner with us and invest money into us. I want a tour bus. I want our sales and influence to grow. I want to feel like we are doing something rather than experiencing failure nonstop.

About a month later my bandmates and I decided that we would try a few more things to give it one last shot: come up with a band name, record a full-length album, and release it. If our fan base still didn't grow, we'd hang it up for good.

Up until that point, we had been touring under the name Brian "Head" Welch. Aside from me, there were only three guys left in the band—Valentine on bass, Dan on drums, and a sixteen-year-old kid named J. R. Bareis on guitar (we found him on Facebook right before we went on tour). My manager didn't want to hire a teenager, but since our original guitar player quit just weeks before the tour, it was either cancel the tour or take J. R., so we hired him. I even signed papers to become his legal guardian on the tour, along with our tour manager Justin Jones. It was awesome because I figured if J. R. messed up on his guitar parts, I could just ground him.

We started tossing some possible band names around, but we couldn't come up with anything we all liked. Then one day—don't ask me why—I was thinking of the two words *love* and *death*. I liked how they blended together because they are two of life's strongest forces. I told the guys about it, and although nobody jumped up and down, they didn't seem to mind it. Just like that, we became Love and Death.

Now we needed an album.

I decided to ask David to call my friend Jasen Rauch, who used to play in the band Red. Jasen had gone into producing full time, and I was hoping he'd be willing to work with me on writing a couple of songs. Turned out he was, and we wrote a song together called "Paralyzed." And you know what? It was one of the best songs I've ever been a part of. It had a crushing, groovy guitar riff that is still one of my all-time favorites. Plus, once I started working with Jasen, I found a good range to sing in, and my voice was doing better than ever. *Finally*. "Paralyzed" eventually went to number one at Christian Rock Radio, and we shot our first music video together as a band with "Paralyzed." Both did very well, and it definitely created some excitement for us.

After the release of "Paralyzed," we saw a big increase in excitement for our music, so we started gearing up to announce the new Love and Death name. Within months we had written a few more songs with Jasen that were absolutely killer. One was called "Chemicals" and another was a revamp of the classic Devo song "Whip It," along with a few other songs we were pretty proud of. A lot of people finally started catching on to what we were doing. That was exciting because after two years of lackluster touring experiences, it felt like God was already answering some of the requests I had written down just a few months earlier.

Right around the release date of our EP "Chemicals," we got asked to go out on tour with Red and Icon for Hire to continue building our fan base. Jennea had already started her online homeschool program, so she hit the road with us. In addition to her schoolwork, I gave her a few jobs to do. Her daily routine went something like this:

- Noon: get up, tweet, text, chat on Facebook
- 12:30–3:30 p.m.: do a little schoolwork, tweet, text, chat on Facebook
- 4:00–5:00 p.m.: hang out, watch the sound check, tweet, text, chat on Facebook
- 6:00 p.m.: help set up our merchandise table, tweet, text, chat on Facebook
- 7:00 p.m.–midnight: sell our merchandise before, during, and after the show, tweet, text, chat on Facebook
- Midnight–3:00 a.m.: finish schoolwork, tweet, text, chat on Facebook
- Go to bed while tweeting, texting, chatting on Facebook

You know, typical teenage stuff.

For the most part Jennea enjoyed touring with us. Having J. R. around was fun for her as well—sometimes. They were almost like brother and sister, and as legal guardian to them both, I had to play referee whenever they'd start snipping at each other.

For example, Jennea caught J. R. talking with one of her friends on Facebook, and man, she was ticked.

"J. R., why are you talking to Carolyn on Facebook?" she yelled.

"I don't know. She friend requested me," J. R. said, shrugging it off.

"Don't talk to my friends!"

"Why? She's cool. I like her."

"Dad!"

"J. R., stop talking to my daughter's friends. It's creepy, dude. You're in my band."

"Okay, okay. Whatever."

You know, typical touring stuff.

In addition to snipping at J. R., Jennea was also starting to mouth off to me. And we were touring in a tiny van that was barely big enough to hold all our equipment, let alone us, so we were right on top of one another all day long. Between the bankruptcy stuff, having to constantly hound Jennea about her homework, touring, and baby-sitting two cranky teenagers in addition to Dan and Val, sometimes I would just snap and lose control.

One day we were leaving a hotel room and Jennea was mouthing off about something I've long since forgotten about, and before I knew what happened, I turned around, grabbed her hard, and yelled at her to *shut up*! My loss of self-control crushed me as I watched Jennea silently cry in the back of the van after we left the hotel. The rest of the band guys awkwardly stayed silent, too, since it was obvious something had happened between Jennea and me.

What was worse, without realizing it I had fallen back into the same old pattern—lose control, flip out with uncontrollable anger, and fall into guilt and depression.

God, I thought I was finally over all these anger issues. Why can't I get past this?

All the responsibilities and heavy burdens I had on my plate were too much for one person to juggle. I was like a steel rod slowly being bent back farther and farther until . . . *snap*!

———

In spite of all the problems, Love and Death's fan base was really starting to pick up. Before we even finished touring, Tooth & Nail Records came on board to back our album.

Finally things were starting to look a little bit more positive financially—and musically as well.

The only thing that wasn't doing well was Jennea. I loved having her with me on the road, but hocking CDs and T-shirts until three in the morning and sleeping in a different hotel every night (if we even got a hotel), wasn't the kind of life a thirteen-year-old girl should have been living.

I tried to spend quality time with her and take her out to dinner and to the movies whenever we had a break in the schedule, but she started pulling away from me. It seemed like all she wanted to do was talk with her old friends from Arizona on Facebook and Twitter. Who could blame her? After all, she spent almost twelve hours a day cooped up in a stank-filled touring van with a few adult male musicians and a teenage boy.

It wasn't ideal, but I didn't know what else to do. I couldn't figure out how to give her the kind of life she deserved. She was slowly slipping away, and it was breaking my heart.

Jesus, things are going so well for me right now musically. The band is doing great. The tour is going great. Our fan base is getting bigger. We've even got a label behind us now. Almost every request I made to you in that letter has come true, so thank you. But I'd give it all up tomorrow if I could just see Jennea happy again. This isn't what I wanted for her. She deserves so much more. I want her to have friends her own age and a normal life, but I don't know what to do. I can't stop touring. We need the money. But I'm afraid if something doesn't change soon, she might fall too far. Please, if there's any way to make the music thing work and get Jennea back and give her the life she deserves, show me what it is. Tell me what to do. Send us some help. Show us a sign. Whatever you gotta do. Just do something. Please.

CHAPTER 7

JUST LIKE OLD TIMES

"Hey, Brian, it's Justin."

"Oh, hey, Justin. What's up?" My band, a couple of crew guys, and I had just arrived in Bakersfield to play at a local bar, and my friend Justin Jones had been managing our latest tour. I figured he had a few last-minute technical odds and ends he needed me to take care of before the show.

"I just wanted to let you know that Jonathan Davis reserved two tables for tonight's show."

What?! You've got to be kidding me! I hadn't seen Jonathan (KoRn's lead singer) in almost eight years, not since I'd left KoRn, and now he was going to be sitting at a little club watching me play? *This is a nightmare,* I thought. *I'm barely scraping by with my vocals as it is, and now Jonathan's going to be sitting there watching me sing!*

Then I remembered. *I'm singing two KoRn songs tonight. Perfect, man. Just perfect.*

I was a nervous wreck. After arriving at the gig an hour before showtime, I was pacing back and forth in the tour bus like a caged animal. I could already feel my mouth turning to cotton. About a million different scenarios flooded my head, each more horrific than the last. *What if I completely botch my vocals, or the mic stand breaks again, or I trip over the amp wires and take a header right off the edge of the stage, or . . . ?*

"Hey, Brian! You in there?" It was Justin. I'd been so busy working myself into a panic I hadn't even heard him open the bus door.

"Yeah, what's up?" I called back.

"There's someone here to see you. Can I bring him up?" he asked, smiling. The next thing I knew Jonathan was standing in the doorway with his wife, Deven.

"Oh man, hey, Head. What's up, brother?" he choked out, coming up the steps.

I couldn't even speak. I just reached out and hugged him.

"Brother, it's so good to see you," he said through tears.

"I know," I said, choking back a few of my own. "I can't believe it's been eight years."

We just stood there, two grown men trying to hold back our emotions. For years I'd wondered what it would be like to see some of the other guys from KoRn again. After Munky's interview came out, I just assumed it was all over. But now, seeing Jonathan again, it was almost as though nothing had changed at all.

Well, *some* stuff had changed.

"Jennea! You are so grown up!" Deven said, pushing her way past Jonathan and me to Jennea, who looked up from her laptop just long enough to notice we had company.

"Yeah, it's so good to see you too." She smiled, pulling out her earbuds and giving Deven a big hug.

"How are the boys?" I asked. "I haven't even met your two sons yet."

"They are so amazing." Jonathan beamed. "Pirate is eight and Zeppelin is five. They are crazy little dudes," he said, laughing.

I laughed back. "Well, I can't wait to meet them!"

"Hey, after the show, why don't we go to my house and hang out a little?" he suggested. "You can meet the boys, and then maybe later we can go to the studio and you can check out our new album."

"Okay, cool," I said. And it did sound cool. If only I didn't have to do the show. Even though seeing him had gone way better than I expected, I was still dreading singing our old KoRn songs in front of him.

That night onstage I was nervous, and it showed. My voice had that shaky thing going on that I hated so much, and I couldn't do anything to stop it. The crowd was good, though, and they didn't seem to mind, which helped. What helped even more, though, was just not looking at Jonathan. I basically kept my eyes closed the entire show.

After the show we went to Jonathan and Deven's house, and when we pulled into the driveway, I couldn't believe it—they were living in Doug and Sandy's old place. Doug and Sandy were the couple who had taken me to church for the first time back in 2005 when I was still strung out on meth. Talk about a small world.

"Dude," I said as Jonathan pulled into the garage, "you're not going to believe this, but I knew the couple who lived here before you!"

"Yeah . . . I know." Jonathan laughed. "I forgot to mention that. A few years ago, Deven and I were looking for a place to buy, and our real estate agent hooked us up with Doug and Sandy. They were really cool. We saw them off and on for a couple of weeks before I realized who they were."

"It was wild," added Deven. "One day we were all sitting around talking, and Jonathan just looked at Doug and said, 'Wait. Are you that guy that took my guitar player to church back in 2005?'"

Jonathan started cracking up. "Yeah, dude. Doug told me, 'Look, I was just trying to help Brian out. He was struggling in a huge way in his life. Anything else that happened, like him leaving your band, had nothing to do with me.'"

We all stayed at the house for a while, and after Deven put Pirate and Zeppelin to bed, Jonathan and I drove over to KoRn's recording studio. Jonathan played me their new album, *The Path of Totality*. It was a little too dubstep and electronic sounding for my taste, but I still liked it, and I enjoyed sitting around the studio, listening to it with him. It was like old times.

"Hey, listen, bro," Jonathan said as we were locking up. "You know your spot onstage is always open if you want it."

It seemed like yesterday Munky and he told Fieldy they didn't want me back after my onstage meltdown in Modesto, California, so this was a surprise.

"Thanks, man. I appreciate it," I told him. "But I'm pretty happy right now doing my own thing."

And I really was happy. Love and Death was nowhere near as big or successful as KoRn, but our audience was continuing to grow. Tooth & Nail was behind us, and I loved being able to meet with and pray for broken and hurting people every night. They all needed God in their lives. They were struggling with pain and depression and addictions, and I'd gone through all that and then some. They needed someone who understood where they were coming from and who was willing to help—without judging them. But the weird thing is, I seemed to be better at helping total strangers than I was at helping my own kid.

Jennea was still having a rough time. Between homeschooling and touring, she still hadn't been able to make many close friends in Nashville. Even though I wasn't a fan of the ridiculous amount of time she spent texting and tweeting with her old friends in Arizona, it did make me feel a little better that she had at least a few girls her age she could talk to. That's why, against my better judgment, I decided to let her take a few trips back to Phoenix to visit some of her friends while I continued to tour with Love and Death.

One night she texted me on the road to ask if I could get her and her friend into a festival near Phoenix that had a bunch of rock bands playing. I had let her go to a couple of shows before, but I didn't feel good about this one. There were way too many people, and I didn't know anyone who'd be there to watch over them. I said no but promised I would make it up to her really soon, and to my surprise she seemed satisfied with that.

As it turned out, "really soon" came even sooner than I expected.

Right around that same time, my booking agent told me about a cool tour being put together with P.O.D. and Red. Those two bands had never toured together before, and I figured Love and Death would make a perfect opener. So I texted my friend Sonny from P.O.D. and asked if he could make it happen:

> Bro, can you get Love and Death on your tour coming up in May?
> We'll do it for cheap. We just need to get out on the road, man.
> We'd love to tour with you guys!

A few minutes later, Sonny texted back:

> Hey, man, let me hit up management and see what I can do.

A couple of days later we were on the tour. It's good to have connections.

While we were preparing for the tour, I found out that Red and P.O.D. were also booked on a couple of mainstream rock festivals that Love and Death couldn't play because we weren't big enough. When I saw the list of bands that were playing, it pretty much mirrored the festival in Arizona that I had just told Jennea she couldn't go to.

Perfect!

I shot off one more text to Sonny.

> Hey bro, would u mind if Jennea and I rode on the bus with you guys
> to the Carolina Rebellion festival? Jennea really wants to see some of
> the bands, and I'd like to take her.

Once again, Sonny texted me back almost immediately.

Sure, no problem.

Thank you, Jesus. That got put together as smooth as butter! Lord, you know how to make a dude smile!

The tour started off great. We played several different venues, and before we knew it Jennea and I were on P.O.D.'s bus heading toward the Carolina Rebellion festival.

Jennea loved the bands that were playing at the metal festivals— Chevelle, Evanescence, Staind, Five Finger Death Punch—her iPod was full of their stuff. She was drawn to all kinds of 1990s music— including KoRn—and I couldn't stop her from listening to it even if I wanted to. If you try to shelter your kids too much, it'll backfire on you. Still, it was hard because even though she was pushing fourteen, she was still my baby. It's a strange thing to watch your child grow into a young adult.

As we got closer to the festival, I could almost feel Jennea's excitement. She was stoked! Me, I was a little nervous. You see, in addition to P.O.D., Red, Staind, and Evanescence, KoRn was also going to be playing at the festival. I'd stayed in touch with Fieldy over the years, and of course I'd reconnected with Jonathan a few months earlier, but I hadn't seen or spoken to Munky since 2005. And given his reaction to Fieldy's suggestion that I rejoin the band, I had no idea how he'd react to seeing me again. So I made a point not to tell anyone I was coming until the day before.

When Jennea and I woke up the next morning, P.O.D.'s tour bus had already arrived at the festival and was parked alongside all the other tour buses. The first thing we did was track down Fieldy's bus.

"What up, man?!" Fieldy said, giving me a big hug as we walked on his bus. "Hi, Jennea. You remember Spider," he said, gesturing toward Pablo "Spider" Silva, who played bass guitar in Fieldy's solo band, Stillwell. "And this," he said, nodding toward rapper Q-Unique, "is Q, our singer."

"What's up, you guys?" I said, reaching over to give Q a fist bump. "Nice to meet you."

Then Fieldy turned back to me. "Hey, we're writing a new Stillwell song. What do you think about laying some guitar on it?"

"Yeah, sure. Let's do it later though," I said, pulling Fieldy aside so we could have a little privacy. "Hey, I wanted to say what's up to Munky. I haven't seen that dude in eight years. What do you think? You think he'd be cool with it? I'm asking because he's been pretty hot and cold about me."

"Yeah, man," Fieldy said enthusiastically. "He's in a good place now. For real. He hasn't had a drink in a couple of years now, and he loves you, man. We all do."

That was like music to my ears. One of the darkest memories of my final year in KoRn—besides my constant meth use—was Munky's constant drunkenness. He would get so drunk that he would literally growl at us. Sometimes he'd even charge at people or threaten to start a fight. It was crazy. And definitely a far cry from the lovable friend everyone adored growing up.

Despite Fieldy's enthusiasm I was still a little nervous as Jennea and I headed toward Munky's bus. As soon as we got there, though, all my fears were erased. Just like Jonathan months earlier, the second Munky saw me, his face erupted into a smile, and he reached over and gave me a big hug.

"Wow," he said, stepping back to look at us both. "You guys look great! Now that I see your face and Jennea's face together and how much peace you guys have in your eyes, it all makes sense."

I was floored.

"Oh, thanks, bro," I responded. "Everything I did, I did for this precious little girl," I said, putting my arm around Jennea. "Well, now she's a crazy teenager, but back then she really was sweet," I said, laughing.

"Wow, thanks, Dad," Jennea said, shooting me a wicked side-glance.

"I'm just playing," I joked. "You're still sweet . . . sometimes." *There. That got a smile out of her.*

"So how old is your daughter Carmella now?" I asked Munky.

"She's eleven," he said. "Man, it's crazy how old these kids are getting. She's a great kid. And she's doing really well in school."

"Man, that's awesome," I answered. "Nowadays we all sound like our parents, saying things like, 'Wow, these kids grow up fast!'" I was joking, but then again I wasn't. It was so strange, thinking about all of us being dads, watching our babies grow up.

"You're so right, dude," Munky agreed. "Well, I'm about to go through that all over again," he said, smiling. "My wife is pregnant."

"What? Are you serious? Congrats, man! That's so amazing!"

After visiting with Munky for a little while longer, Jennea and I left to let him get ready for his show and to catch some of Jennea's favorite bands.

As we watched Chevelle, Staind, and Five Finger perform, a strange thing started to happen. I started to get really emotional as I looked out into the crowd. I've been to a lot of music festivals, and let me tell you, fighting back tears while watching metal bands just isn't normal. All of a sudden, I felt this overwhelming sense of God's love for all the people out there. It was like God was whispering to my heart, *These are my people, and I want them.* It was so intense.

I was snapped back to reality by KoRn's tour manager, Jens.

"Hey, Brian. Jonathan is up now if you want to see him before the show."

"Yeah, definitely. Thanks," I said, herding Jennea back toward the line of tour buses. I was looking forward to seeing Jonathan again. We'd had such a good time a few months before, and I wanted to hang out a bit since I was there at the festival.

"He should be out in just a minute," Jens said. "Have a seat." Jennea and I plopped down on one of the couches in the front of Jonathan's bus and waited for him to come out. When he finally did, I could hardly believe my eyes. He looked terrible. He must have lost almost fifteen pounds since the last time I saw him. He was gaunt, pencil-thin, and almost zombie-like. I tried to play it off like everything was perfectly normal, but I knew something was up—and it wasn't good.

A few minutes later, Munky and Fieldy came in, and the three of them sprang something on me that I hadn't expected.

"Come on, Head," said Fieldy. "Come to the meet and greet with us to meet some fans."

I turned to look at Munky.

"Yeah, come with us," Munky agreed.

Huh. What is this all about? I wondered.

To be honest, it felt a little weird because I'd been gone for eight years. But I went ahead and did it, and it was really cool hanging with the guys and meeting some fans.

As showtime approached, I grabbed Jennea and headed backstage to wish the guys luck before heading out into the crowd to watch from the audience. That's when Fieldy hit me with the next surprise of the evening.

"I'm just sayin'," he said, smirking and gesturing toward the stage. "There's a guitar and an amp up there for you if you want to jam with us."

"Ah, man, I want to watch you from the crowd. I don't want to play," I shot back.

"Then just jam a few songs with us. Just do our old radio hits at the end of the set."

"Nah, I don't even remember those," I said. Then I thought about it for a second. "But my solo band plays 'Blind,' so maybe I'll just jam that," I offered.

"Cool." Fieldy agreed.

So instead of going out to the crowd to watch them play, Jennea and I ended up standing backstage for the entire show, waiting for them to get to "Blind." It was almost as if I was dreaming, but in a good way. I'd had so many really negative dreams about KoRn over the years, and now here I was getting ready to play with them. Live. Onstage. In front of thousands of fans.

Lord, what is going on here? I just came here to chill out and say hi to a few old friends. And here I am getting ready to hit the stage with KoRn? This is crazy. This feels very weird, but cool.

By the time they got to "Blind," I had changed my mind after discussing it with Fieldy during one of his breaks between songs. Not about playing, but about how I was going to walk out onstage. If I was gonna do this, I was gonna do it right. So instead of just stepping out from the shadows, I went over to the other side so I could walk all the way across the stage when Jonathan introduced me.

It was so surreal. The crowd was cheering, and Jonathan gave me a huge intro.

"You know, for a long time this spot right here has been very lonely," Jonathan said, standing exactly where I used to stand onstage for eleven years before I left the band. "Very, very lonely. I wanna bring out one of my truest and oldest and most beloved old friends to come out and have some fun with us." Then he turned in my direction and screamed, "My boy!"

I suddenly got a picture in my mind of me holding the guitar over my head as I walked out, so when Jonathan shouted me on, that's exactly what I did.

The crowd went wild!

"You guys ready to get crazy?" Jonathan screamed. "This is where it all began, people! Are you ready?!"

As soon as the first few bars started playing, the whole place went bananas. I was losing my mind from all the energy. All the inner conflict I had battled with before about whether or not I should play with them vanished. And for around four minutes, while we all jammed and Jonathan sang, it felt exactly like old times.

At one point I looked over on the side of the stage and noticed that all the other bands who had played earlier in the day were right there cheering us on. When the song was over, Jonathan gave me a huge embrace and then broke down in tears. He had to ask the crowd to give him a minute before they finished the set because he was so choked up. And Jonathan wasn't the only one. A lot of people out in the crowd were in tears. It was very emotional.

Even Jennea got caught up in the moment.

"Dad, I'm not even kidding," she blurted out excitedly when I met her backstage. "That was so rad!"

"Really?" I asked. "Thanks, Nea," I said, fighting a lump in my throat.

That evening had been so incredible, I didn't want it to end. Unfortunately, P.O.D.'s tour bus was getting ready to leave, so Jennea and I had to go catch a ride with them to continue on with our P.O.D./ Red/Love and Death tour. It was back to reality for me as I was meeting up with my Love and Death bandmates the next morning.

"Later, J. D. I love you, man. That was so much fun!" I called out into Jonathan's bus as we left.

"Okay, Headly," Jonathan said, hurrying over to give me one last hug. "Whether we ever do anything else in music together again or not," he continued, "at least I have tonight, so thank you, brother. Thank you very much."

"That's so cool of you to say," I said. "We'll talk soon, man. Love you."

We said our quick good-byes to Munky, Fieldy, and a couple of other guys, and then Jennea and I made a mad dash to the tour bus, which was idling impatiently in the lot.

As Jennea and I settled in and the bus pulled away, I put my head back and tried to cement everything that had happened that day into my memory. This had been one of the most surreal experiences of my life, and I wanted to truly take it all in. Yet later that night when the adrenaline wore off, I started to feel torn inside. I'd had the time of my life playing with KoRn out there, but there was a reason I'd left eight years ago. That "reason" had been struggling a lot lately—at school, with friends, even with me. For Jennea, I had tried so hard to steer clear of the whole metal lifestyle—the drugs, the depravity, and the dark, sometimes depressing lyrics. How could I even think about going back? Then again, after tonight how could I not?

I ended up talking to Sonny about it for a while on the bus, and he gave me an insight I hadn't considered.

"Listen, man. I think the rock world is exactly where Jesus needs us," he said. "Think about it. We may be the only picture of Jesus most of those fans will ever see because they won't step foot in a church."

My mind raced back to that afternoon when Jennea and I were watching Staind, Chevelle, and Five Finger perform.

These are my people, and I want them, I felt God whisper to my heart.

Is this what you were trying to tell me, God? Do you want me to go back? Sonny's right. We may be the closest thing to Jesus a lot of these people ever see. But what about Jennea? She's going through such a rough time right now. She's the reason I left KoRn in the first place. What would happen to her if I went back? Please help me process all of this in a healthy way.

CHAPTER 8

BACK WHERE I BELONG

"Well, I guess Love and Death is over," said my bass player, Val, with a smirk as I stepped off the bus to find him standing there, smoking what was most likely his twenty-fourth cigarette of the morning. "You're going back to KoRn, aren't you?"

"Shut up," I said, waving a cloud of smoke away. "And get that smoke out of my face." I laughed and changed the subject. "Come on. Let's go sound check." The truth was, I didn't know what I was going to do, and I was in no mood to talk about it. But everyone else was.

"Well, well, well," said my drummer, Dan, as Valentine and I walked into the club where the sound crew was setting up. "I can't believe we weren't at the show where you jump onstage and play with KoRn for the first time in, what, eight years?"

"Look. I didn't know it was gonna happen," I said, laughing. I wasn't going to let these guys goad me into anything. "How was I supposed to know they were gonna invite me onstage to play?"

"Well, if you go back to KoRn, you'd better bring us with you," Dan joked.

"I'm not going back to KoRn," I said flatly. "You guys are idiots. Now come on, let's sound check."

The rest of the tour went pretty well, and after a few weeks all the Internet insanity over the big KoRn reunion died down. I didn't hear from Munky, Fieldy, or Jonathan the rest of the tour, so I tucked the experience away. By the time the tour wrapped up, Jennea and I were both exhausted and anxious to get back home to chill for a while.

And chill we did. Actually, I chilled in Nashville. Jennea went to my parents' house out in Bakersfield to spend some time with them and her cousins.

I wasn't even home a week when something extraordinary happened. I was listening to some instrumental spiritual music that helps me focus on the reality of the spiritual world, along with some teaching messages about Christ's glory, and I suddenly felt that familiar, tangible presence begin to come all around and inside of me. It was so strong and so consistent, and an overwhelming feeling of being caught up or taken into another realm surrounded me, as if dozens of angels were in my house. It felt like I was literally drunk with a love that can't be experienced from the earth—something only tapped into through Jesus in the spiritual dimension. It was so real.

The whole experience lasted about a month, which was longer than any of my previous experiences. Truly like heaven on earth.

It was during that time that I got the phone call from Munky.

"You know, we're hitting the studio soon to start writing for our new record," Munky said a few minutes into our call. "What do you think about coming down and trying to write with us? See what happens?"

"That's cool," I said. "But I don't think it's the right time for that now. I just signed a record deal with my other band. Thanks for thinking of me, though, bro."

"Well, I just want you to know that it's great to be connected to you again either way." Then he added, "Just think about it. If you change your mind, let us know."

"Will do. Thanks, man, really. It's so great to be talking with you again," I said. And I genuinely meant it.

Tempting as it was to take Munky up on his offer, there were a few issues that I just couldn't reconcile. One of them was Jonathan. He was not in good shape in his personal life, and I knew it. A drug abuser knows a drug abuser, and that dude was abusing drugs. I didn't know what kind, but I knew it was something. I was not worried about myself slipping back into drug use. I was and still am done. Completely. Free in every way. But I didn't want to come back into a band where there was drug abuse going on right in front of me.

I tried to let the whole idea go and get on with my life, but for some reason it kept popping back into my head. I fought it for a couple of days, and then I decided I should do the smart thing and talk to God about it.

God, this isn't going away. KoRn seems to be everywhere I go. No matter what I'm doing, KoRn is there in my face in one way or another. I ran away from it, and now here it is again. What should I do? Could this be you doing something here?

Eventually I came up with what I considered to be a foolproof plan.

I decided that I would call the band's managers and tell them that if I'd ever consider coming back to KoRn, there'd be a few things that would have to happen before I agreed to it. I figured there was no way they'd agree to everything I asked for, and that would be the end of it.

See? Foolproof.

I was brimming with confidence when I called Jeff Kwatinetz, KoRn's manager.

"Hey, Jeff, it's been a long time," I said.

"Hey, buddy, how've you been?" he asked. "It's great to hear your voice."

"I'm good, man. I've just been raising my daughter for the last few years. Now I'm wondering if maybe this KoRn thing is supposed to happen. It's wild," I said, laughing. "I've been runnin' away from you guys for eight years, and now here we are."

"Well, we love you, bro," Jeff assured me. "We'd all love to have you back."

Here goes, I thought.

"Well, I have a few questions. I have this new band, Love and Death, and we just signed a record deal. We need to tour, so if I came back, would it be cool for us to get on the KoRn tours like Fieldy's band has in the past?"

"Sure, bro, that's no problem," Jeff said without so much as a pause. "We can definitely make that happen."

"Okay . . . cool," I said, caught a little off guard. I hadn't expected him to agree to that so quickly. "Well, as I said, I've been raising my daughter for the last eight years, and I've given my entire life to Christ, so there are one or two songs that I'd rather not play. It would just be awkward for me as a dad, ya know?"

"Bro, of course. You guys have dozens of songs, so everyone can bend a little to compromise. Whatever makes everyone happy," Jeff responded.

Whoa. I did not see that coming. Apparently my plan wasn't as foolproof as I thought. Or was it? In the end, Jeff agreed to every other request I brought up.

Maybe this call with Jeff was the sign I'd been waiting for.

But just to be sure, I decided to seek out the advice of a few other people. The first was Pastor Ron from the church in Bakersfield where I had first met the Lord.

"Hey, Brian, great to hear from you!" Pastor Ron said as soon as he heard my voice. "How are you doing?"

"I'm doing good. Something has come up though. KoRn has asked me to come back," I explained. "And this time, their managers have agreed to my requests, and to take my solo band on the road with them. Got any advice for me?"

I was totally unprepared for his answer.

"Brian, Debbie and I have been praying that you'd go back to KoRn for a while now. This is your family. There are so many of your fans that hate the thought of Jesus because of coldhearted religious people. You can help change that if you go back."

"Wow," I said, genuinely taken aback. "I'm not sure I expected to hear that from you." I paused for a second. "I think maybe it's time though. Things are lining up perfectly."

"Well, we back you 100 percent, Brian. If you need anything, just call."

One down, two to go.

Next, I called my friend Nicole Miethe. She and her husband, Hayden, were great friends of mine. I first noticed them at an event in Nashville right after we moved to town. They were hard to miss because they looked wild like me with lots of tattoos and funky hair. Hayden even had one of those big ole beards like the *Duck Dynasty* guys, which is pretty funny because he's also a rapper in a band called Vinyl Jones and the Domestic but doesn't look like the typical rapper-type. They're also involved with media like me. In fact, when we met, they were shooting the pilot for their forthcoming reality show about their family (complete with *eight* children) to various networks.

Anyway, Nicole has one of the strongest spiritual gifts I've ever witnessed. She hears, sometimes shockingly, accurate words of destiny for people from God's Spirit. I thought it would be a good idea to run the whole scenario past her to see what she thought. I told her about the Carolina Rebellion concert, the conversation I had with Sonny, and the call I'd had with Jeff.

"I feel like all the pieces are lining up," I said, already knowing that of all people, Nicole would completely understand where I was coming from.

She agreed. "This has destiny written all over it, Brian. You could be such an incredible influence on people. I feel really good about this. God is doing so many different things that are outside of the normal church mentality nowadays."

Okay, that's two.

The last person on my list was my dreadlocked, tattooed pastor friend, Clint. Clint pastored a church in Nashville called SlowBurn, and I'd been going there for a couple of years. I thought he'd be in favor of me going back to KoRn, but after I brought him up to speed on the situation, he told me that he didn't feel like it was the right time—which is what I initially told Munky.

Hmmm.

"I could totally see it happening someday, buddy," he said. "Just not sure that the right time is now."

I took it straight to God.

Lord, I really felt like I needed three different friends that I trust to all confirm that going back to KoRn would be a good call. But Clint has come back saying he's unsure if now's the right time. I really don't feel comfortable moving forward with this yet. What do you want to do from here?

Take note: this may seem weakminded on my end to some people, but the foundation of God's entire system is humility, and in the spiritual realm these types of actions regarding big decisions carry much weight and significance.

About a week later I went out to my birthday lunch with Nicole, Hayden, and Clint. As soon as Clint arrived at the restaurant, he came right up to me and said, "Hey, buddy, I gotta tell you, I've been praying a lot about what we discussed and the more I think about it, the more I'm starting to feel good about the timing of it all. How are you feeling about everything?"

Before I could respond, Nicole chimed in. "Clint, we feel the same thing. This is what Brian was created for. The circumstances are all falling into place for him."

"Definitely," added Hayden. "Brian, I think this is exactly where people like us need to be. Churches are full of people being fed spiritually, and a lot of them hardly do anything to make any impact. Things like this need to happen."

"I agree," I added. "I've been seeing this direction open up ever since I got onstage with the KoRn guys. But it sure feels good to have all of you backing me up."

This was turning out to be one awesome birthday.

I felt so good inside because I really started to own my decision in my heart about returning to KoRn after talking to my friends. And I needed to feel extremely strong inside about it because I knew I would face a lot of naysayers throwing mud at me over the decision in the near future.

Right after lunch, someone forwarded me an e-mail from a girl named Jennifer, who saw me play "Blind" with KoRn at the Carolina Rebellion festival. She was wasted at the show, but when she got home, God reached out to her and touched her. Here's what she wrote:

> The day Rebellion started we were back at our tent grabbing some beers before going back over to the venue, and we were handed a flyer for a free event in Charlotte, which one of the bands at Rebellion was going to be playing at. Brian "Head" Welch, the ex-guitarist of KoRn, and his new band were playing in Charlotte also. Actually, KoRn was also playing at Rebellion, and I had never been a fan since Brian had left. So when I saw that he was going to be at this event, I was in! Well, to my surprise, at the end of KoRn's set, Brian Welch reunited and played with them for the first time in eight years. Well, this all intrigued me so much that as soon as I got home I ordered his

autobiography and dived in, which is saying a lot, because I hated reading even something as short as magazine articles!

I cannot find the words to begin to describe the feelings that flushed through me reading his life story and all that God had done for him. I completed his book on the nineteenth of May and went to bed with so much weighing on my mind. I woke up the next morning, Sunday, May 20, 2012, and went to church for the first time willingly in over twenty years. I no longer had any fight left inside me and no one else to turn to but God. I had Brian "Head" Welch's book *Save Me from Myself* held tightly to my left side, as close to my heart as it could be. For through Brian, God had brought me to this church of complete strangers, knowing I was supposed to be there.

I found the chair farthest away from people, closest to the back, wanting to be noticed and not at the same time. The entire drive there, I told God that he had to give me a sign that I was really supposed to be there. Once I got there, I began to plead with him to send someone to me, because I didn't have the strength to find someone myself. In actuality, I was scared!

Well, of course, he spoke to me through the pastor's sermon. So, of course, I sat and listened. Then the end came, they all prayed, and boom—church was over. I dropped my head in defeat feeling even more alone. I just began to beg him to send someone to me and then told myself that if no one came to me, I would wait until I no longer heard any voices, and then I'd leave when no one could see me, because that is exactly how I felt—invisible—and now, even more unwanted than I had ever felt before in my life. I was confused as to why God had done so much to get me there, yet was not sending anyone to me.

Finally, with only a handful of people left in the Sanctuary, a woman placed her hand on my back. I cried, relieved that I wasn't invisible, and that he heard me and sent someone to me. In fact, it was the woman's twelve-year-old daughter who saw me and told her mom to go and talk to me. Pauline began to talk to me to see if she could help me or figure out what was wrong. She then went to find whoever she could to come and talk with me.

Thanks to God sending me Brian and his story and for sending me Pauline. That morning, around 12:15 p.m., with Pauline at my side, the pastor led me in prayer to accept the Lord into my heart and SAVE ME!

As I sat in my car after lunch in the parking lot just outside of the restaurant and read Jennifer's letter, everything clicked for me—any doubts I had left in my mind finally vanished right then and there. Through Jennifer, Jesus showed me a picture of what he was going to do with countless other fans. I was completely floored and humbled, and I sat there in my car in tears at the thought of how good, non-religious, and nontraditional God's wild ways are.

There was just one more person I needed to talk to—Jennea.

Over the years, whenever KoRn's managers would reach out to me about coming back, Jennea had always been the one to say, "No, Dad! Don't go back in KoRn!" And who could blame her? I wasn't exactly winning father-of-the-year awards back then. Not only was I away from home a lot, but I was also so strung out on drugs that even when I was at home, I was never fully present. Besides, when I left I had told Jennea it was so that we could spend more time together. If I were to go back, what kind of message would that send? Still, she was older now and a lot more independent. And she did get a kick out of seeing me perform onstage with KoRn again.

There was no use putting it off. Jennea was still at my parents' house, so I gave her a call and just came out with it after a few minutes of small talk.

"Nea," I began, "since Carolina Rebellion, I've been talking to the KoRn guys about possibly coming back. What do you think?" I held my breath.

"I think it would be awesome!" Jennea said, sounding genuinely excited.

I have to admit, I was a little surprised—again.

"Well, you always said no way over the years, so why do you think it's a good idea now?" I asked.

"You saw them, Dad," she said. "Everyone is happy now, and sober. Love and Death plays music that sounds a little like KoRn anyway, so I think it would be great. Besides, they're your best friends."

She had a point. Things were different now. I was still concerned about Jonathan, but everyone else seemed to be doing really great.

I breathed a deep sigh of relief. I wasn't sure if Jennea's enthusiasm was because she really thought it was the right thing to do or if it was because of all the free concerts and festivals she'd get to go to. But either way, I was glad she was fully on board.

That night I texted Munky, Jonathan, and Fieldy so we could set a date for all of us to get together at KoRn's studio in Bakersfield.

Hey, I talked to Jeff. Looks like this is gonna actually happen!
This is crazy. Let's set a date soon to jam, cool?

Within minutes, all three of them texted me back.

I love you, brother. This is amazing; I can't believe this is happening. I feel all giddy, lol.—JD

Right on, man, can't wait!—Munky

Yeah, man!!!—Fieldy

Since we were all eager to get started and KoRn's studio was in Bakersfield, where Jennea was already staying with my parents, I hopped on a plane a few days later. I don't know what I was more excited about: jamming with the guys or seeing Jennea sooner than we had originally planned.

When I got there, my parents were almost as excited as I was. That made sense. They had known the KoRn guys for more than twenty-five years. They were like family. In fact, my dad told me that the day after I made my surprise appearance onstage at the Rebellion festival, he saw the video online and was so overcome with emotion that he shed some tears. I took this as one more sign that this was the right thing to do. That felt pretty amazing.

It got even better the next day when we all met at the studio to start writing. As soon as I walked in, I noticed guitars, amplifiers, and all sorts of musical instruments and equipment sprawled all over the place. It was just like I remembered it: messy and dark—exactly what a rock-and-roll studio should look like.

"Man, this place is a wreck," I joked.

"Yeah, but it's all ours," Munky said.

"True," I agreed. "It's got a great vibe to it." It did bring back memories.

"I remember recording vocals for 'Ball Tongue' with Jonathan and our producer Ross for our first album back in 1994 in this same exact room," I reminisced. "We made Ross take us on a drug run without him knowing it, and when he found out, he was fuming!" I couldn't help but chuckle at how stupid I used to be. Man, I'd come a long way since then.

As we stood around talking and laughing about the old days, it was almost as though not a single day had passed. Eight years later, the connection between Munky, Fieldy, and me was just as strong as it had ever been.

A few minutes later, Ray showed up. David Silveria, the original drummer for KoRn, had left the band back in 2006, and Ray was the new drummer. I was looking forward to working with him, mainly because of his positive personality and attitude.

"What's up, guys? You ready to rock this?" Ray said with a big smile.

"Yeah." I reached out to shake his hand. "I'm so stoked to work with you. I've heard a lot of great things about you from these dudes."

"Oh, right on, man," he said, nodding. "I really appreciate being in this situation. Believe me, I don't take it lightly. I've always wondered what it would be like to sit back and watch four original KoRn members going nuts in front of me while I play the drums."

When we started jamming out our first song idea, everything clicked just as it always had, but better. Having Ray playing with us was very refreshing. David was awesome back in the day, too, but Ray really helped me feel relaxed. I also quickly learned that he had all kinds of funny David Lee Roth (Van Halen) impressions from touring with Roth for eight years, so that was a bonus.

Nothing, however, could compare to the musical connection I felt with Munky. There's just something that happens when Munky and I play guitar together. It's like we're twins or something. Everything he plays blends perfectly with what I'm doing, and vice versa. And Fieldy's bass has always gone beautifully with our style. He and Ray were doing ridiculous tricks in the rhythm section from the start. It was a great jam session, and by the end of that first week, we all knew that it was all gonna work out great.

The only strange thing was that Jonathan only came to the studio for about five minutes in the beginning, and then he was MIA for the rest of the time. Since his issues were one of the only lingering concerns I had about coming back to the band, I decided to call him and see where he was, health-wise and emotionally. I'm glad I did.

"Hey, brother," he said, sounding exhausted. "I'm sorry I can't come down. I need to detox from these prescription pills I've been taking. I've been addicted to Xanax and some other medications. Plus, my son Zeppy was just diagnosed with diabetes, and I'm freaking out. I just need to get better, bro."

"I've been there. You know that," I said. "Listen, I'll be praying for you. You get yourself better. We need you."

I wished there was something more I could do for him, but I knew the best thing I could do right then was pray for him and trust that everything would work out.

In the meantime, Fieldy, Munky, Ray, and I got together off and on and recorded all kinds of song ideas for our new record. We'd usually jam out for three or four days and then come back the following week. After the second week we'd take a break and then come back a month later. Every so often we'd all flock to my parents' house for dinner. My dad is famous for his tri-tip steak, and my mom makes some killer side dishes, so we were eating like kings. Fieldy's mom and stepdad also lived in Bakersfield, so we'd eat there too. It was seriously just like old times. In fact, with the exception of Jonathan's absence, things couldn't have gone better. Then one day, out of nowhere, I got sick with the flu, had a little panic attack, and started questioning whether I was making a huge mistake. It was weird. It was like panic fell out of the sky and landed on me all of a sudden and I was like, "What am I doing back in KoRn?!"

I texted Nicole, and she called me right away and prayed for clarity. In the end, I figured it was just the flu making me feel confused, and after talking with Nicole I could see clearly again that I was doing the right thing.

One bad day didn't mean I was going in the wrong direction. It just meant I was having a bad day. I really should have been thankful I'd only had one bad day because Jonathan was having dozens of them.

And lately Jennea was having a few of her own.

I knew she was having trouble during our Love and Death tour, and I was hoping that spending a few weeks away from all of us at my parents' house might help even things out a bit, but it didn't. She was still spending far too much time holed up on her own, texting and tweeting her old friends from Arizona. Plus, over the past several weeks, I had noticed a definite shift in her attitude toward me both in person and on text.

We started butting heads more than ever before, and we got into some really horrible fights. In the last chapter of my book *Save Me from Myself*, I wrote about the shouting prayers I had with God when I was going through an especially trying emotional time, and I mentioned a dark moment when I actually screamed "F—you" to God. I also wrote that if Jennea were to ever say anything like that to me, I would forgive her so fast, just as God forgave me.

Well, I was about to live that out in real life.

One afternoon while Jennea and I were back in Nashville, we got into it over . . . actually, I can't even remember what we were fighting about. I just remember that I was really stressed out trying to juggle music, traveling, financial untangling, being a single dad, and staying on top of Jennea, her schoolwork, and her chores. More often than not, I'd choose the wrong words or say something in the wrong tone, and it would set her off. (She gets that from me, by the way.) One day our bad moods collided, and in the middle of a heated argument she got up and stormed out of the house. I ran outside after her and yelled at her to get back in the house. Then, instead of defusing the situation with love, I said something I probably shouldn't have, and that's when she hit me with it.

"F—you!" she screamed.

"What did you say?" I asked, my entire body tensing up.

She paused for a second and then buried her face in her hands and wept. I think she was every bit as shocked as I was to hear those words come out of her mouth. I also think it overwhelmed her a little to realize just how badly our relationship had deteriorated.

I wish I could say that was the worst of it, but it was only the beginning. We had so many fights back then, it was hard to keep track of them all. Pretty much anything could set us off. Sometimes just me messing with her too much—trying to be funny—would start a fight.

It all started here; the house in Phoenix I purchased for me and Jennea. This photo was taken just before I had the weird looking tiny walls and landscaping put in.

Jennea with her new bike, wearing her cute little Freedom Academy school uniform just after we moved into our house.

Jennea doing her Steve Urkel impression—
Family Matters being one of our
favorite Nick at Night shows back then.

2006

Don't you just love the cheesy
backgrounds they used to come up
with for school photos back in the day?

PHOTO COURTESY LIFETOUCH

Here I was, sitting all confident right before I stepped out of the limo to hit the *High School Musical 2* red carpet event . . . CRICKETTS!

"Um, it's . . . um . . . um, it's . . ." Jennea
froze as Isabel stepped in to answer the DJ's
question, live on air with Radio Disney.

I have never seen Jennea's face look this bashful since she met the two main stars (Zac and Vanessa) of *High School Musical 2* that day.

The creepy photoshoot that Edgar and I did with the impoverished looking Croatian kids.

I will never, ever forget the day I experienced Jesus walk into my room. He will visit anyone who radically pursues him for nothing else but to simply know him. Motives must be pure.

Meet Ocean—the bear Jennea named and brought home right after I had a vision of myself floating in an ocean. Ocean is chillin' on a painting by the amazing Rolando Diaz.

Jennea and "Queenie Brown Fudge Welch." How could I say no to that face?

This is cute, adorable, preteen Jennea—before the storms came that rocked us both to the core.

Me, Val, J.R., and Dan riding the subway and doing some press in NYC for our debut Love and Death album.

Jennea's favorite band Blink-182. This concert was an amazing memory we got to share together just before the dark clouds arrived.

Enter the rebellious teen years. The hair started off cute and fun, but I soon lost my little girl to the self-hate and depression that is unfortunately an epidemic for her generation. (Bottom left: Amy Lee from Evanescence with Jennea)

Masks. We all wear them well, don't we? This is Jennea and me smiling and posing for the camera during the most gut-wrenching holiday season of our lives. I dropped her off at Awakening Youth just days after this photo was taken.

This photo says it all. It was so emotional my first time playing with KoRn again that JD was in tears, along with many others.

After deciding that going back to KoRn was meant to be, we got together to jam and had some steak at my parents' house.

I have no idea why TMZ decided to run a story about me getting "a Hebrew tattoo on my Christian face."

PHOTO COURTESY KELLI PUTMON

About a year after my bankruptcy, I visited the courtroom where I was accused of fraud and grabbed a victory photo!

A heart and soul painfully broken. An angel risen from the pieces. There is no father on earth prouder than I am.

PHOTO COURTESY ANNA MAY PHOTOGRAPHY

I have made so many mistakes. But the mistakes involving my daughter hurt me the worst. God is healer. God is forgiveness. God is love. These genuine smiles are proof.

PHOTO COURTESY ANNA MAY PHOTOGRAPHY

Dancing with the angel at her graduation celebration.

The beautiful girls from Awakening Youth.

PHOTO COURTESY ANNA MAY PHOTOGRAPHY

Photos from a few different states after KoRn's concerts on our tour with Slipknot. Fieldy and me leading fans to the most important decision of their lives.

PHOTOS COURTESY KURT FAUST

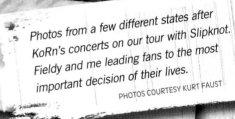

This is what it's all about. It's why I do what I do.

Or we'd fight because she wouldn't do her schoolwork, or because she was spending too much time on her phone or on Facebook.

Man, the Facebook thing again. It drove me crazy. I had begun to suspect particular girls weren't helping the situation. And then there were the boys—some of whom she didn't even know. They were just friends with her other friends. I had made it clear to Jennea that I didn't want her talking to boys until she was older, but she insisted that they were only friends, so I let it slide. Sometimes I was just a pushover. Big mistake.

One day while Jennea was in the shower, I noticed her iPhone sitting on her nightstand. When I picked it up, I saw a trail of, let's just say, extremely inappropriate text messages.

I was quickly losing control of the one person I trusted God to keep closest to himself. It felt like my insides had been ripped out. I couldn't hold my emotions together, and the tears started falling. *Where did I go wrong? Why am I such a failure as a dad?*

I was completely devastated. I think it really freaked Jennea out too. When I confronted her with what I'd found, tears streaming down my face, instead of getting all defiant like she usually did, she rushed over, wrapped her arms around me, and started apologizing profusely.

"Dad, I'm so sorry. I'm so, so sorry. I won't ever do it again. I promise. Please don't be upset." Then she started crying.

At that moment everything I had asked God to do for my daughter over the years seemed like empty, unanswered prayers. I was so confused, but I had to make a serious choice. Would I be so offended that I'd shrink away from God? Or would I trust that he would answer all those prayers in his timing?

I chose to trust and wait patiently in my pain and confusion.

In the meantime, I made it abundantly clear to Jennea that she was, under no circumstances, to have any contact with the kids she was texting—ever again. Needless to say, that ultimatum did nothing to improve the atmosphere around our house.

For the remainder of 2012, our lives consisted of traveling from our home in Tennessee to Bakersfield, where I continued to work with Munky, Fieldy, and Ray on KoRn's new album. Jennea traveled with me, and while it wasn't all doom and gloom, that dark cloud over her head always seemed to come back. It was so painful to watch her sink lower and lower into depression. I tried to talk to her, but I never seemed to have the right words to say. I always seemed to make matters worse.

We talked about getting her into counseling, but she was dead set against it.

"No, Dad. We can work this out. I'll be okay. I just need some time," she would argue.

I so wanted to believe her, and for a while I did. Until one day I noticed something different about her arms.

She had started cutting herself.

That was the limit. Like it or not, she was going to counseling. I had tried having her talk to a counselor a couple of times shortly after moving to Nashville because she was having trouble connecting with other kids her age, but the counselor hadn't felt like a good fit to Jennea. So, as I had done so many times before, I went to Jesus to find out what to do.

God, I need help with Jennea. I need help quick!

Take note: a lifestyle of continued communication with God always produces results.

A few days later I was texting a friend of ours named Wendy, asking for advice, and out of nowhere she had a revelation.

Brian! I cannot believe I didn't think of this until now! I think I have someone for Jennea to meet who may be a big help!

Really? Fill me in.

I have a friend named Cristi who is a counselor. I think she would be
perfect for Jennea to talk to! Here's her number.

Okay, thanks!

Filled with new hope, I wasted no time in getting ahold of Cristi.

"Hi . . . Cristi?" I started. "This is Brian Welch. Wendy gave me
your number and said you might be able to help me with my daughter,
Jennea."

"Hi, Brian! Nice to meet you." She sounded very sweet. "So did
Wendy tell you anything about me?"

"No, not much," I answered. "Just that you counsel young people
mostly."

"Yeah, I work with a lot of young adults. I actually fly to LA a lot
and work with a few teens in the entertainment industry."

Well, I thought, *that helps.*

"I work in LA, but I live here in Nashville. I've toured with my
daughter and her friends in their band when they were around Jennea's
age, so I'm really looking forward to meeting you two."

"Yeah, us too." Now she had me curious. "What band is your
daughter in?" I asked.

"Paramore," Cristi said.

Whoa! Paramore was one of Jennea's favorite bands.

"Awesome! How soon can you see us?" I asked.

We made an appointment for early the following week. I was so
excited. Not only did Cristi specialize in working with teens in the
entertainment industry, but she was the mom of the lead singer of one
of Jennea's favorite bands. If Jennea was going to let anyone into her
life to help her, Cristi would be the one. Once again, God's hand was
all over our circumstances, and for the first time in months I started
to feel like everything was going to be okay.

The first counseling session went pretty well, but it was clear we still had a long way to go. Jennea believed lies about herself and about me, and they clouded her view of reality.

"Jennea, do you believe that your dad loves you?" Cristi asked about halfway through our session that first day.

"No, I don't think he loves me," Jennea answered sternly. "I think he only cares for me because he has to."

Ouch.

"You don't think I love you?" I replied, flabbergasted. "How can you say that? I left my entire career to take care of you. My whole life revolves around you. I do love you; it makes no sense for you to say that."

Jennea sat silent and shrugged her shoulders. I looked over at Cristi, who was giving me a look that said, *It's okay, stay calm. I've got this.*

"Jennea, what goals do you have for your life at this point?" Cristi asked, momentarily defusing the tension in the room.

"Well, I wanna get one of those old vans and live in it so I can tour with my own band all the time when I'm old enough," she answered.

"Jennea, I'm sorry," I interrupted. "But I have much bigger dreams for you than touring in an old van. Besides, I don't want my daughter living out of a van as a homeless person."

Cristi and I tried to speak into Jennea's life about all the future greatness she was capable of, but Jennea's walls were built up so high that no quick fix was going to break them down. I was frustrated by what I'd heard, but I had to quickly learn to celebrate the small victories; at least Jennea was willing to talk to Cristi. That was a huge step. The ironic thing about all this was when I was around Jennea's age, my mom put me into counseling for being distant from our family, and I acted very similar to how Jennea acted in Cristi's session.

Before we left, Cristi put together a plan. Since we would be traveling back and forth between Nashville and Bakersfield for a few more months, Jennea would start doing weekly Skype appointments with Cristi. Amazingly, Jennea was open to that.

Cristi also had a plan in place for me.

"Brian, if things don't start to get better soon, or if she starts harming herself again, we're going to have to hit the nuclear button and get her some serious, long-term help, okay?"

"Got it," I told her. "Here's hoping it doesn't come to that."

Over the next few weeks, things started to turn around. Jennea and Cristi kept up with their weekly Skype sessions, and I prayed that we'd be able to make it through all the difficulties without having to push the nuclear button. But just in case we didn't, I started working on a plan B.

I had a friend named Tiffany who had been running a boarding school program for at-risk teens called Awakening Youth with her husband, Travis, and her mom and dad, Dee and Dean. I first met Tiffany and Travis at one of my solo concerts back in 2011. They had brought a bunch of kids they were working with to our concert because a couple of them were fans of mine. The cool thing was, I ended up meeting all the kids after the show, and they actually prayed for and encouraged me more than I encouraged them. Jennea got to meet all of them, too, and she had a great time—though she did mention to me that she could never be in a boarding school like those kids.

"Dad, if you ever tried to put me in a place like that, I would definitely disappear," she said, matter-of-factly. "I'd run away for sure."

Good to know.

Every once in a while after a big fight between me and Jennea, I would call Tiffany up and ask for advice. But after Cristi mentioned the nuclear button, I figured it couldn't hurt to call Tiffany to ask her about her school and if she might have any openings the following year.

"Hi, Tiffany. It's Brian," I said, trying to sound upbeat. "How are you guys?"

"Hi, Brian. We're good," she answered. "How are things going with Jennea?"

"Well, it's challenging, but we do have some decent days with no blow-ups, so that's good." Then I decided to come straight out with it. "I've just been thinking . . . if things get worse, what would you recommend? Would you have any openings next year if it came to that?"

"Well, it's hard to tell because we have a couple of new girls coming in at the beginning of the year," she said, sounding apologetic. "But we could discuss it in more detail if you really get serious about it."

"Okay, well, I was just wondering," I said. "I have her in counseling right now. Things will probably be okay. I'm just trying to put a back-up plan in place. You know. Just in case."

I really did believe that Jennea would be okay and that she wouldn't need to be sent off anywhere for more intensive therapy. I held on to that belief for dear life. After all, things were going well with Cristi, and the holidays were right around the corner. Jennea always loved going to my parents' house for Christmas, and with everything going so well with KoRn, I had every hope that we would both have a great Christmas.

Little did I know, we were all about to experience the most difficult Christmas we'd ever had.

CHAPTER 9

GOING NUCLEAR

In 2005 I walked away from a successful music career so I could spend more time with my daughter. Now it seemed like the more time Jennea and I spent with each other, the worse our relationship got. In just under seven years, I went from Super Dad, who brought home pet hamsters, took her on dream vacations to Disneyland, and made it possible for her to meet her favorite TV stars, to Stalker Dad, who was constantly looking over her shoulder, reading her text messages, and monitoring her Facebook posts.

Even though I was doing it because I loved her and was worried about her, like most teenagers Jennea saw it as an invasion of her personal privacy. She was trying so hard to grow up, and I was trying to keep her my little girl for as long as I possibly could.

Over the years I'd encountered hundreds of broken young people holding on for dear life through the songs I'd written or the words I'd spoken. I'd seen darkness piercing through their eyes, and it was heartbreaking every time. But now here I was seeing that same darkness staring back at me through Jennea's eyes. I felt completely helpless.

Coming to the realization that your own child hates herself is one of the worst pains a parent can feel. We want our kids to be confident and happy. We don't ever want to worry about whether they'd do anything to injure themselves—or worse. I'd been through a lot in the past seven years—bankruptcy, depression, betrayal, slander, professional failure—but watching Jennea slowly slip away from me, God, and herself was the most painful experience of my entire life.

Around that time Pastor Clint invited me to come with him to Bethel Church in Redding, California. I was excited to go—mainly because a lot of great music comes out of there, like the artists Jesus Culture, Brian and Jenn Johnson, Steffany Gretzinger, Jeremy Riddle and Amanda Falk, and others—but my excitement dimmed when Jennea started cussing me out via text after I arrived, telling me she hated me because of my problems with her inappropriate Twitter messages. I was at my wit's end, struggling to be loving but firm as we texted back and forth and, at the same time, wondering how in the world we would get through this.

But God always knows just what we need. He lifted my spirits in that difficult time, and he did it through the most unexpected person.

"Brian Welch? Is your name Brian Welch?" An older woman in her eighties approached me during the service at Bethel.

"Yes, ma'am, nice to meet you," I answered, wondering how she knew who I was because ain't no way Grandma could have been a metal fan!

"I've been reading your book," she explained. "Last night the Lord woke me up in the middle of the night to pray for your daughter."

Wow. I was floored. There was no way she could have known the turmoil simmering beneath the surface, and I was completely blown away by this expression of God's loving encouragement.

The next day Pastor Chris Overstreet from the church found me in the crowd and walked up to me.

"Brian, God just spoke something serious to me," Chris said, looking directly into my eyes. "You're going to have a new daughter in eight months."

What? How?

Good luck with that, God.

I thanked Chris but turned away, struggling to believe that statement, yet still trying to. It was a lot to take in. I'd been getting cussed out via text message by Jennea all weekend, and though I appreciated the encouragement, the reality of our situation seemed worlds away from the message I'd just been given. But in the end I chose to believe the message anyway. Months later I realized that I could confidently rely on that prophetic word.

The next day I arrived in Nashville and picked up Jennea from our friend Wendy's house. Things had calmed down a bit by then, but I was still wondering what type of blow-up would come next.

As much as I hated to admit it, the counseling sessions Jennea was doing with Cristi were more of a Band-Aid than a long-term solution. With every passing day and every little fight, I began worrying more and more.

Then one day I realized Jennea had started harming herself again.

We were battling back and forth about the usual stuff—school, chores, Facebook—when I noticed a fresh set of cuts on her arms.

"Jennea," I started, "Cristi and I told you that if you didn't stop hurting yourself, we'd have to get you more intensive therapy."

I could see the lack of concern in her eyes.

"I won't do it again, Dad," she said, rolling her eyes.

I wanted to believe her, but we'd played this broken record before.

"You have to tell Cristi that you're hurting yourself again at your next session," I told her.

"Why?" she asked, her eyes glazing over with tears. "I said I wouldn't do it again."

No dice. This time, I needed her to take responsibility for her actions no matter how uncomfortable it felt.

"Because that's what she's here for, Nea. Either you tell her, or I will."

To her credit, Jennea did have the conversation with Cristi at her next appointment. As for me, after talking with Cristi myself and discussing it with Jesus, I picked up the phone and made the call I'd been dreading for weeks. It was time.

"Hi, Tiffany," I said, trying to control the emotion in my voice.

"Hey, Brian. How's everything going?" Tiffany said, sounding happy yet a little concerned to hear my voice.

I just put it out there. "Listen, Jennea isn't getting any better. In fact, she's started hurting herself again." I took a deep breath. "If it's possible, can we figure out a good month to get Jennea into Awakening Youth later next year? Maybe in August after KoRn finishes our summer tour."

I heard Tiffany release a big sigh.

"To be honest with you," she started, "I've been thinking about this a lot. I've worked with girls in this situation before, and unfortunately, my opinion is it's only going to get worse from here— especially if you add in the unstable lifestyle of touring. If you wait until August, she'll most likely be too far gone for me to take her into our program."

She paused for a second, I think expecting me to say something in response, but by this point I could barely even think straight. That's when she threw me a lifeline.

"I know I mentioned before that we were booked up, but it looks like we'll have an opening in the beginning of January after all. So if you decide you'd like to take the spot, let me know as soon as you can so I can hold it for her."

It was decision time. I knew Jennea would have loved going out on tour with KoRn and seeing all her favorite bands play all summer, and I would have loved to have made that happen for her. But deep down, I knew Tiffany was right. Things were going downhill fast. I needed to get her some serious help—now.

I had given Jennea the best upbringing I knew how, and we'd had a lot of great times, but through this opening in Tiffany's program, God was showing me he was her Father before me. It was time for him to take over. It was time for him to heal the deepest places of hurt inside Jennea and start preparing her for her next phase in life.

I took one final breath and said, "Okay. Let's do it. Let's get her in right after the first of the year." I had never felt so relieved yet so defeated at the same time.

I knew that enrolling Jennea in Tiffany's program was the best thing I could do for her, but that didn't make the decision any easier. In fact, it all but killed me. I could hardly sleep at night because of the anxious thoughts attacking me like a plague. In the course of one phone call, I had gone from spending all summer with Jennea to shipping her off to Indiana while I went on tour without her.

I kept hearing the words, *"Dad, if you ever tried to put me in a place like that, I'd run away for sure,"* echoing in my head.

I knew this was the right thing to do, but I still had a huge case of the what-ifs.

What if I was wrong?

What if I was damaging our relationship even more?

What if, after the eighteen-month length of the program, Jennea came out unchanged or worse than when she went in?

I needed help. I needed proof that this was 100 percent the right decision. I was 99 percent sure; I just needed that final 1 percent to put everything into motion.

So I called Nicole.

"Brian," she said as soon as I explained the situation, "I've been praying about this, and I really feel this is meant to be. I am telling you, I see an incredible new beginning for Jennea. Not only is God taking you to the next phase in your destiny with KoRn, but he is preparing Jennea for her own life, calling, and destiny. I know it's difficult and painful, but your decision is going to help launch her into a new existence and bring out the young woman that he is preparing her to be."

Wow! The storm inside calmed down right after hearing those words. Nicole was right. I knew sending Jennea away would crush her spirit and break her in a way that she had never been broken before, but deep down that's what needed to happen. How could she get put back together unless she was completely broken with nowhere else to look but toward Jesus, and nowhere to run except to him?

By this point Jennea wanted nothing to do with Jesus. She had been around different churches and Christians since she was six years old, but after she watched all the disasters I had gone through with Edgar, the lawsuits, the repos, and the bankruptcy—not to mention all the Christians bashing me online for my tattoos and for still playing heavy metal—she wanted nothing to do with Christianity. She knew Jesus was real and not some figment of our imaginations, but seeing her own dad go through so much while loving Jesus most likely turned her off to Christianity.

Nicole was right. Getting Jennea away for a while would be the best thing not only for *our* relationship but for her relationship with God too.

So that was it. The date was set. I was to bring Jennea to Tiffany's and Travis's place on January 7, 2013. Now all I had to do was get through the holidays confrontation free. Easier said than done.

I wanted to tell Jennea that I'd enrolled her in Awakening Youth so she could have time to prepare herself mentally and emotionally. But I was afraid that if I did, she'd run away like she had threatened to. So I just played it cool. Well, as cool as one could play it under the circumstances.

For the next few weeks, we were like oil and water. Jennea did the exact opposite of everything I said. It was like *Clash of the Titans*. I was going into her Facebook account and seeing things like, "My dad's trying to control me. He says he's gonna take away my computer and make me get help because I'm hurting myself, but he's not gonna do anything."

Oh, is that right? I thought.

As much as it hurt to read things like that, it also made me that much more sure I was doing the right thing. Not that it made it any easier.

Jesus, you have been so good to me, but you've also made me face the most difficult battles I've ever faced. This one is the worst. I've always prayed that you would keep Jennea close to you, and lately it feels like you've abandoned us. She is getting worse and worse. I know you are helping us by getting her into Awakening Youth in January, but Christmas is coming, Lord, and things are spiraling out of control. I need your help now. We both do.

"So, are you ready for Christmas, Nea?" I asked as we started the two-hour trek by car from LAX to Bakersfield.

"I guess." Jennea shrugged, texting away on her phone.

Yeah . . . this is gonna be a fun drive.

My parents' condo had always been a peaceful place to spend the holidays. They lived on a golf course, so it was a quiet and relaxing environment. *Please, let it stay that way,* I thought as we pulled into their driveway.

As soon as we walked in the house, Sandy, my parents' Maltipoo, jumped all over us. It was the first time I'd seen Jennea smile or heard her laugh in a while. *Maybe things will be okay after all.*

And things did go well—for the first two days. Then the Facebook stuff started up again.

Jennea knew I had full access to her Facebook account, but somehow she thought I'd forgotten about it—or she was just trying to mess with me. Either way, she started sending inappropriate comments back and forth with her friends again. I read everything she wrote to one kid in particular, and to his credit, he was trying to stop it so Jennea wouldn't get in trouble again. But for some reason Jennea didn't care.

The last thing I wanted was to have a big blow-up with Jennea at my parents' house—especially at Christmas—but I couldn't turn a blind eye and let her do whatever she wanted. So I confronted her.

"Jennea, I don't know if you think I'm stupid or just don't care anymore," I said firmly, "but I checked your Facebook account, and I know you're acting trashy with your friends and talking to that one kid again after I asked you not to. You promised me you wouldn't. Why would you do that?"

"Sorry. I wasn't thinking," she said in a tone that showed me she really didn't give a rip.

I closed my eyes, took a deep, cleansing breath, and started counting to ten in my head. I made it to six before Jennea apologized again, though halfheartedly.

In order to avoid a full-blown war, I told her I would be taking her laptop and phone away for a couple of days, and if she chilled out and listened, I would give them back. I'd decided it was best to try to work out a compromise.

For the next few days Jennea did seem to make an effort. Granted, it probably had more to do with wanting to get her stuff back than anything else, but at least things had calmed down for a while. So, true to my word, after a couple of days of decent behavior, I returned them.

"I'm giving these back under one condition," I said. "No more trashy behavior, and stop talking to that kid, do you hear me?"

"Yeah," she mumbled.

Maybe now she'll get that I'm serious, I thought.

Guess what—surprise! She didn't.

That afternoon, I went up to the guest room to check on her, and I opened the door to find her typing away on you-know-whose Facebook page.

But that wasn't what ultimately sent me over the edge. What pushed my nuclear button were the familiar scabby, dried-blood marks peeking out from under her shirtsleeves. But I also noticed something else that reduced my feeling of anger and raised my level of concern; some of these blood marks weren't dried yet. The blood was new. My heart sank.

"Jennea, let me see your arms," I said as calmly as possible.

"No," she shot back, pulling her sleeves down over her wrists.

"Jennea, I'm serious. Let me see your arms."

"No, Dad. Just leave me alone." And with that, she turned up the volume on her MacBook, and Blink-182's "Always" filled the uncomfortable silence between us.

"I told you," I started again, my entire body starting to tremble. "I told you what the rules were, and you keep breaking them over and over."

"But, Dad . . ."

I quickly cut her off. "Jennea—no. That's it. This whole social media thing—it's over for you. You're cutting this thing off right now. No more Facebook."

"You don't get it!" she spat back at me, standing up. "My friends are the only ones who make me feel like I don't want to kill myself!"

Man. What are you supposed to say to *that?*

"Nea," I said, attempting to comfort her.

She instantly pulled away. "Just leave me alone." And with that she turned her back on me, hugging her laptop to her chest like a security blanket.

Maybe that was the problem. Maybe I *had* been leaving her alone too much. It's not like I thought a couple of weeks at my parents' house would make up for all the time we'd been apart lately.

How did everything go so wrong so fast? I wondered.

Jennea's shoulders started to shake, and I could hear her starting to cry. It was about all I could do at that point not to break down myself. I slowly made my way around to the other side of the bed, and, as calmly and gently as I could, said, "Jennea, please. Let me see your arms."

She didn't budge, so I reached over, took her left hand in mine, and pulled back her sleeve. When I saw the trail of horizontal slash marks running from her wrist to her shoulder, a wave of nausea rolled over me.

Oh, God, what could possibly be so horrible that she would do something like this?

I felt like an utter failure. Again.

I was at a total loss. Not only did I not know how to respond, but because it was so close to Christmas, I had to do something fast. I couldn't just let her continue to tear her arms apart. And the comment about wanting to kill herself scared me to death.

I racked my brain. Where could I get Jennea help right away out here in California? Then it hit me—Pastor Ron.

"Hi, Pastor Ron? It's me, Brian," I said, trying to keep the panic out of my voice and failing. Then I just unloaded. "Listen. I'm at my parents' house, and Jennea is in a really dark place. She's been really depressed, and right now she's in full-on rebellion mode. She's talking crazy online, cutting herself, and she said she wants to kill herself. It's not just a cry for help. I know my kid, and I've never seen her go through anything close to this. There's a boarding school I'm sending her to in January that will help her, but I really need to get through

Christmas. I want to get her out of the house before my parents see her bloodied arms. Can you help me? Please?"

"Oh man, Brian. I'm so sorry you guys are going through this. Let me think for a minute," he said. "I'm going to hook you up with one of my best youth leaders. His name is Brad, and I'm sure he'll be able to help Jennea."

Frankly, I wasn't sure anyone short of God himself was going to be able to help Jennea at this point. But I was desperate, so I had Pastor Ron set up an appointment for us to meet with Brad that same day.

Ten minutes into the meeting, as Brad sat there, covered in tats and telling Jennea about his rough background and his "screamo" band, I thought, *Hmmm . . . maybe this guy* can *get through to her.* But Jennea wasn't impressed at first. In fact, she barely looked up from her phone through the whole meeting. *Welcome to my world, buddy,* I thought.

"Now what?" I asked Pastor Ron privately in a separate room. "We can't go back to my parents' house. If they see the marks on her arms, they'll flip out."

Pastor Ron stared at me for a minute and then rubbed his face and said, "Tell you what. Debbie and I have a ranch up in the mountains that the church uses for retreats. Why don't you and Jennea go up there for a few days? It won't solve any problems, but at least it will give you both some time to calm down before Christmas and hang out at a peaceful place. The only thing up there is nature and my animals."

"Oh, that sounds awesome!" I said, finally feeling some of the intense pressure lift. "I'd much rather hang out at the ranch for a few days and then call my parents to tell them about Jennea's bloodied arms so they have time to process everything before Christmas."

I wasn't sure that Jennea and I spending time alone together at a ranch in the mountains was the best idea, but it sure beat going home and facing my parents with the news that their granddaughter had been contemplating suicide. Fortunately, we had secretly brought our bags with us before we left my parents' house, just in case Brad and Ron decided we needed to take Jennea somewhere else immediately. By that time Jennea was texting back and forth with Brad a little bit because we had gotten a CD of the screamo band he was in and she actually liked it—which helped her open up to him a bit more. He was also trying to throw in some encouraging texts to her, and that helped, but she was in too much of a dark place for any quick changes.

Soon after we got to Pastor Ron's ranch, I called my mom to tell her where we were—and why.

"Hi, Mom, it's me," I said, trying to sound upbeat.

"Hi, Brian," she responded. "Are you all done Christmas shopping?"

Oh, yeah. I had almost forgotten the excuse I used to get out of the house earlier that day.

"I think so," I said. "Jennea and I are up in the mountains right now. Pastor Ron has loaned us his house, and we're gonna be staying up here for a couple of days."

"Oh." She paused. "Okay."

"Listen, Mom. I want to prepare you for something," I said. "I know I told you that Jennea has been struggling a bit lately, but it has gotten worse—a lot worse. She's hurting herself, and it's gotten pretty bad. She has cuts all the way down her arms, from her shoulders to her wrists."

I heard my mom gasp.

"I know that the first reaction is to freak out, but I've been talking to a friend of mine named Tiffany who runs a boarding school out in Indiana. She has seen this kind of thing countless times, and she says the best thing to do is to keep a close eye on Jennea's safety, and although it's emotional for us, she says we should try not to draw unneeded attention to the cutting—overreaction could escalate the behavior.

"I've already enrolled Jennea at the school in January. She'll be there for at least eighteen months. She doesn't know about it yet, and it's important that she doesn't. She's threatened to run away if I ever tried to put her in a place like this. I've been praying about it though. I've talked to a lot of people, and I really believe that this is God's plan."

Mom was silent for a second, and then she blurted out, "Eighteen months? She's going to live there full time? Are you sure this is the best thing?" I knew what she was worried about. It was the same thing I was worried about—leaving Jennea for an extended period of time, just like I used to do back when I was touring with KoRn.

"Mom, this is meant to be," I said. "Jennea's gonna be a legal adult in three and a half years, and this place will help prepare her for when that time comes. Touring with KoRn full time will in no way be beneficial for Jennea."

Mom sighed. "Okay, Brian. It just kills me that she feels this badly about herself. She is such a beautiful, intelligent girl. I wish she could see that."

"She will, Mom. She will," I said with more confidence than I felt at the moment. "It's just gonna take time. I'm not about to let my little girl fall apart. I'm doing everything I can to see her completely healed. And I'm being led by Jesus, so I know things will be okay, even though it's really scary right now. Will you talk to Dad for me? Let him know what's going on?"

"Of course I will," she promised. "You take care of yourself—and Jennea too. See you in a couple of days. We love you both."

Considering what I had just unloaded on them, my parents ended up taking everything extremely well. They agreed to take Tiffany's advice and not bring any attention to Jennea's injuries. If we didn't focus on it, then hopefully Jennea wouldn't do it anymore—or at least as much as she had been. I also asked my mom to call Jennea's aunt and uncle, who we'd see on Christmas Eve, and fill them in on what was happening in case they noticed the cuts on her arms.

In the meantime, Jennea and I tried to make the best of our time away from the world.

Pastor Ron's cabin was actually pretty cool. He had a couple of cows and horses that Jennea and I fed, which was fun—especially the horses, because they had these huge teeth, massive gums, and huge lips that flapped all over the place when they ate. At Ron's advice, we also carried a baseball bat outside with us just in case a mountain lion attacked, which he had seen lurking around a few times. It was definitely an escape from the norm.

Some moments helped us forget about the war that was going on, but there were also darker moments. Jennea had sent another inappropriate message to a friend on Facebook with her phone (yes, I gave it back to her for the sake of peace), and when I confronted her about it, she totally snapped on me.

"Jennea! Why are you talking like that on Facebook again?" I firmly asked.

"Get a life, Dad! And get off my Facebook account!" she screamed back. "You're such a control freak! I hate you!"

You could practically smell the Christmas spirit.

We yelled back and forth, and then things escalated a bit; she came after me and punched me in the back as I turned and walked away, leaving her to scream out her rage. When I got to the bedroom, I flipped on the television, found a good crime drama, and turned up the volume until I couldn't hear her screams anymore. *At least someone has a more screwed-up family life than me*, I thought as I dove into the TV show about murder and whatever else.

On Christmas Eve, we left Pastor Ron's place and headed back to my parents' house. Though there was still some tension between Jennea and me, things had brightened up a little bit with the promise of Christmas and presents looming on the horizon. It didn't hurt that every year we went to my Aunt Deia's and Uncle Tim's house with a bunch of our extended family, so Jennea got to hang out with her cousins.

We all exchanged presents and had our annual Mexican potluck dinner, and Jennea got what she always requested at that time in her life—iTunes gift cards. So for the moment, she was content. We had a pretty good time, and it did help lift the heavy load we'd been carrying that year—if only for a few hours.

On Christmas morning my parents woke up Jennea and me around eleven. Lots of drama makes you extra sleepy, I guess. My brother, Geoff, his wife, Lola, and my nephews, Max and Sam, had already descended on my parents' house, and the kids were anxious to start unwrapping their presents. My mom had mentioned the cuts on Jennea's arms to Geoff and Lola, but we didn't tell Max and Sam because they were too young. That morning, however, Sam, the youngest, noticed the cuts, and curiosity got the best of him.

"Hey, what happened to your wrists?" Sam asked innocently.

"I fell on my skateboard," Jennea said uncomfortably as she yanked her sleeves down over her hands.

Definitely a bittersweet Christmas morning.

Getting through the holidays at my parents' was hard enough, but getting through New Year's was going to make Christmas look like . . . well, Christmas. Don't ask me how, but I let Jennea talk me into letting her visit some of her friends in Arizona. Since so many of her issues were attached to this circle of friends, I didn't want to let her go. But at the same time I felt like I had to since they were also the only real friends she felt she had. We agreed that she would stay at her friend Bridget's house. I was pretty good friends with Bridget's mom, Syra, so before Jennea left, I gave her a call.

"Hi, Syra. It's Brian, Jennea's dad," I started. "I wanted to call and tell you a little bit about what's been going on with Jennea these past few months. There's no easy way to say this, but she's been really depressed, and she's started experimenting with self-harm."

"Oh no," Syra responded, sounding genuinely concerned. "Why is she so depressed?"

"Well, it's a lot of things, but I'm getting her some help after the first of the year," I said. "Can you please just keep an eye on her while she's there? I'm sure she'll be fine because she'll be having fun with Bridget and her other friends, but I just wanted to take extra precautions."

"Of course, Brian. No problem," Syra promised. "I'll make sure she has fun."

In the end, Jennea did have a good time with her friends, but she still struggled a bit. I was keeping up with her through Facebook, and she'd write things to certain kids that were not cool for a dad to read, so we still had a few clashes here and there.

I also checked in with Tiffany while Jennea was away.

"Brian, you've got to let go and to stop checking her Facebook page," she said firmly. "It's only going to drive you crazy and hurt both of you even more. As difficult as it may be, you have to try to keep the peace until she enters Awakening Youth."

I knew she was right, but I couldn't stop being a dad. And somehow, by God's grace, both Jennea and I made it through the holidays. I would need every bit of that grace, though, to get me through what was coming next.

———

January 7, 2013. The hardest day of my entire life had arrived.

Instead of flying her straight home to Nashville, I told Jennea I wanted her to meet me in Chicago, where I had a speaking event booked a few days earlier. The only thing I mentioned to her was that we were going to visit a boarding school in Lafayette, Indiana, on our way back home. She didn't ask many questions, which was good.

After I picked her up at Chicago O'Hare airport, we drove to Lafayette, got a hotel room, and settled in for the last night we'd spend together for a while. I was an emotional wreck inside, but I didn't show it. Jennea had been pretty quiet on the drive, opting to blast her new Blink-182 album as opposed to talking. But once we got to the hotel, she opened up a little.

"Dad, what's next for us?" she asked.

Whoa. Communication? As I watched her carefully wind up the cord to her earbuds, I realized for the first time how much she resembled me—both inside and out. Though her hair still showed traces of her latest dye job—kind of a festive Christmas green, but way brighter—the resemblance was obvious.

Jennea and I both had our own unique way of expressing ourselves. With me, it was tats and dreads. For Jennea, it was dying her hair all sorts of wild colors. In the past year alone, her hair had been dark purple, lavender, magenta, pastel pink, deep blue, light blue, gray, and now green. We both loved the same kind of music. We were both crazy night owls, and we both loved being out on the road. We also shared a lot of anger and insecurity issues. We both battled depression from time to time, and we both had our share of struggles with self-harm. For me, it was drugging and excessive drinking. For her, it was physically hurting herself. The only thing we didn't share at the moment was a deep faith in God and the unwavering belief that he was going to pick up all the broken pieces of our lives and make everything okay. Man, how I wished we had that in common.

"Nea," I said, brushing my dreadlocks out of my eyes. "Let's just take one day at a time and trust God to lead us."

The next morning came quickly. Too quickly. After wolfing down a quick Starbucks breakfast, we piled into the car and headed off toward Tiffany's and Travis's school. When we got within a mile or so, I decided it was time to bite the bullet and tell Jennea a small piece of what was about to happen, but not the entire truth—yet.

"Jennea, remember that couple who had all those kids with them from the boarding school that came to the Love and Death show?" I asked, staring straight ahead and gripping the wheel way tighter than necessary.

"Yeah," she said, still clueless, scooping the whipped cream up from her grande vanilla Frappuccino.

"Well, that's where we're going," I said, glancing at her out of the corner of my eye.

She shot me a suspicious look. "Why?"

"I just thought we'd check it out," I said, trying to play it cool so she wouldn't figure everything out and make a run for it.

"Whatever," she mumbled, turning to stare out the side window.

Once we got there, we got out of the car and rang the doorbell, and a couple of college-aged students came to the door and invited us in. Then Tiffany and Travis appeared.

"Hey, Brian! Hey, Jennea! It's so good to see you both," Tiffany said, giving us each a hug.

"It's good to see you too," I said.

"Hi," Jennea answered as she stood there, frozen, eyes darting around the room.

"Why don't we head downstairs so we can talk?" Travis said, breaking the awkwardness.

I have to admit, it felt a little weird being in that house—mostly because it seemed too small for so many girls. Tiffany must have read my mind because she quickly mentioned that they were planning on purchasing a piece of property that used to be a nursing home so they could expand. The house was only temporary.

"Travis, why don't you take Brian out to see the new property?" Tiffany suggested. "Then Jennea and I can talk."

Jennea shot me a quick deer-in-headlights look, and I instinctively took a step toward her, but before I could say anything, Travis spoke up. "Sure. Come on, Brian. Let's give the girls a little time to check out the place." And with that he led me up the stairs, leaving Jennea and Tiffany alone.

When Travis and I got back to the house about forty-five minutes later, Tiffany greeted us as we stood at the top of the stairs.

"Brian, why don't you come on down? I'd like to talk with both you and Jennea," she said, pointing Travis toward the kitchen.

As Tiffany sat down, Jennea stood behind her, quietly yet frantically mouthing and hand signaling to me. *No way. I will not go to this school. Let's leave.*

I was a little nervous that Jennea might try to make a run for it when I told her she was staying. But I knew that Travis was upstairs, so that helped with most of my nervousness.

"Come on over and sit down, Jennea," Tiffany calmly suggested.

Jennea, not wanting to be rude, did as she was asked, and Tiffany started telling us more about the school.

"So the program is eighteen months and even though it is hard for you to imagine now, almost every single girl ends up loving it, or at least appreciating the value of the experience by the end," she said, shooting reassuring glances back and forth between Jennea and me.

"We work with a limited number of students at a time. This gives us the opportunity to tailor a program that is individual to each student and her family. We create an environment and culture that allows for students to regroup, heal, and find who they really are. There is a lot of travel, music, art, and new experiences to be had. We don't push God. We allow for a therapeutic environment of peace, and in that we get to watch him build a relationship and bring about change in their lives as we work with them on school, family, teen issues, and overall life. We also do group sessions and discuss all the issues that young women go through in society and culture. And no subject is too controversial or shocking to discuss. If it's an issue in one of the girl's lives, we'll deal with it head-on; this includes interpersonal issues among the group—everyone has a voice. But if it were a private matter, I would do a one-on-one session. Every student is different in her emotional, spiritual, and social capacities. We assess where the girls are and take them from there to where they are going. The huge benefit of a residential approach is that I will really get to know both of you and be available as situations are actually occurring."

Jennea didn't look convinced.

"How many girls do you have enrolled right now?" I asked.

"We have fourteen right now, but we are looking to expand a bit when we relocate," Tiffany answered.

I could obviously tell that Jennea wanted nothing to do with this place, and it didn't look like Tiffany's description of Awakening Youth was changing her mind, so after Tiffany gave me the go signal by nodding her head, I decided to come out with it and hit Jennea with the cold, hard truth.

"Jennea, we're not here to visit," I said, my heart pounding in my throat. "I'm enrolling you today. You're staying here."

Jennea jumped up out of her chair. "No! I'm not staying here! F—that! F—you!" she cried. She looked around for an exit, but Tiffany took control.

"Jennea, you need to sit down," she said steadily. "Calm down and relax."

"I don't have to listen to you!" Jennea cried.

Now I was the one frozen in my tracks.

Tiffany pulled up a chair. "You either sit on the couch or sit in this chair, but you need to sit down somewhere."

Defeated, Jennea sat down in the chair and started crying angrily. My heart shattered into a million pieces. I saw the fear and shock in my little girl's face, and it all but killed me.

"You have two choices," Tiffany continued. "You can either calm down and accept the choice your dad has made to enroll you here, or I will be forced to enroll you in a more restrictive program for a month, after which I will *think* about letting you come back here."

Whoa, I thought. *She really knows what she's doing.*

"Your dad has given me the authority to help him in your family's situation," Tiffany continued. "I don't want to have to call a transport service and have them take you to another program, but I will. It's up to you."

That was it. It was over. And Jennea knew it.

I knew I was doing the right thing, but I was dying inside. I had never known pain like this before. The only thing I can compare it to was when I had to take Jennea to the doctor as a baby and hold her down while the doctor stuck a needle in her. In both instances she was sick and needed to get better. And as her dad, I was just doing what needed to be done to make that happen.

"Brian, can you go upstairs and give us a few minutes?" Tiffany asked, snapping me out of my trance. "There's some paperwork that needs to be filled out before you leave anyway. Dee will be up there to help you."

After walking through the most intense few minutes of my personal life, I knew it would be very beneficial for Tiffany to have a few minutes alone with Jennea. She had to lovingly, yet sternly help her submit to the difficult beginning of the process. And to be honest, I was grateful. I couldn't bear seeing the look of hurt and betrayal in Jennea's eyes one second longer.

It took fifteen or twenty minutes to finish all the paperwork, and by the time I got back downstairs, Tiffany had already snatched Jennea's most prized possession out of her hands—her iPhone. And with it went any and all connection Jennea had to Facebook, Twitter, Instagram, or text messaging.

I could read Jennea's face like a book. She knew her life would never be the same.

"Jennea," Tiffany gently said, "give your dad a hug good-bye. It's time for him to go."

Jennea walked over to me, latched on, and started sobbing uncontrollably.

It.

Was.

Brutal.

"I'm sorry." Jennea slowly hiccupped in between sobs. "I'm . . . really, really sorry, Dad."

"Jennea, I will never abandon you," I promised her, my voice shaking. I completely lost it. Tears flowed down my cheeks and onto Jennea's shoulder. It was almost more than I could bear.

I was there when Jennea took her first breath. I was there on her first day of preschool. I was there when her mom left. I was there from first through eighth grade, and now part of me felt like I was letting her down. Still, deep down, I knew everything was unfolding the way it was meant to. I knew God was in control and that he would bring healing to Jennea, to me, and to us.

"Bye, Jennea. I love you," I said through tears.

"Bye, Dad," Jennea said with the saddest, most broken voice I'd ever heard from her. "I love you too."

And with that Tiffany led me back upstairs while the college students sat with Jennea.

"She'll be fine, Brian. I promise," Tiffany said, trying to reassure me. "What you just did was as hard as it gets."

I wanted to believe her. I wanted to believe that everything was going to be okay. That Jennea was going to be okay. That this wasn't the biggest, most epic mistake I'd ever made. There were a million emotions, thoughts, and questions running through my head, but when I opened my mouth, all I could say through my flowing tears was "I gotta go."

"Are you going to be okay?" Tiffany asked as I opened my car door to leave.

"Yeah."

That was it.

It was done.

And so was I.

The next three hours driving back to Chicago alone were the longest I'd ever experienced. I don't think I stopped crying once.

The road from Lafayette to Chicago is almost completely flat and straight. It was freezing cold, and the sky was a gloomy steel gray— exactly the way I was feeling inside.

"God, I trust you" were the only words I could speak during the three-hour drive as the road stretched out before me.

By the time I boarded the plane to Nashville, I was completely spent—physically, emotionally, and spiritually. My being couldn't handle anymore. As soon as I settled into my seat, I passed out.

When I got home, I put my key in the lock and slowly opened the front door. The house was dark, cold, and silent.

Just like me.

CHAPTER 10

WHAT GOES DOWN, MUST COME UP

I refuse to give up.

When life knocks me down, I come back swinging. It's okay to cry. To feel the sting of the wounds that life brings. To hold the pain of your worst suffering close to your heart until it grows wings and transforms into a blessing from God—the kind that only he can bring. Never in a million years will I let the weight of any strangling pressure cut off the life flow that comes from inside of me.

The same Spirit that raised Jesus from the dead lives in me and Jennea, and because of that, I knew things could only go up from the depths we found ourselves in.

Jesus, please help Jennea accept the program at Awakening Youth. That's all I ask right now. Just let her accept it and grow from here. The last thing I want her to do is beg me to take her home. It'll crush me.

I was strong, but I was still hurting, so I decided to let my pain form words that would move God's heart to perform miracles in our lives. God lives forever because he is love, and love can never die. We all need to learn how to let that sink in.

God.

Is.

Love.

He doesn't just love us. Love is what God is. When we say prayers that come from a place of love, his heart is moved and love pours out of him. It brings about radical change right before our eyes. I had seen it happen countless times before, and I knew that if I continued to pour out my heart to Jesus, it could and would happen again.

And yet, I missed my daughter.

By rule, communication with Jennea had been very limited for the first few weeks after I dropped her off at Awakening Youth. According to Tiffany, the healthiest way to transition the girls to their new environment was to limit the amount of communication they had with their parents until they adapted to their new schedules, rules, and surroundings. It killed me not being able to talk to her every day, but I couldn't argue with Tiffany's success, and I certainly didn't want to do anything to get in the way of Jennea's progress and healing.

Though I couldn't speak to her on the phone for thirty days, Tiffany kept texting me with updates, which I appreciated a lot. I was also allowed to write to her, which I did often. I even wrote her a poem.

> Sometimes,
> *No matter how many tears flow,*
> *Good-bye is mandatory,*
> *In order to grow.*
> I love you, my daughter . . .

Jennea wrote me letters, too, but I have yet to read them. As part of the program's protocol, Tiffany reviewed all written communication, and she told me the letters Jennea wrote during that first month were mainly her trying to persuade me to take her out of Awakening Youth. She wrote meaningful apologies and promised that she had changed, but I told Tiffany I didn't want to read them; they'd only break my heart. I couldn't handle having my little girl beg me to take her home. No matter how much I missed her and wanted her home in Nashville with me, I knew Jennea couldn't leave Awakening Youth—not yet anyway. I had to be strong and keep reminding myself that the brutal situations we had been through—the horrific fights and dangerous self-harm—couldn't just change overnight.

In addition to the no-phone-calls rule, I wasn't able to visit for two months, which was the longest I'd gone without seeing Jennea her entire life. It was difficult but necessary. The text updates that Tiffany sent me every few days helped a little, but it didn't make it that much easier, especially when some of the updates involved Jennea crying and telling Tiffany she wanted to come home.

Tiffany also sent me photos of Jennea, some of which were taken within hours of my dropping her off. It turned out, right after I left, Tiffany and a couple of the older girls took Jennea to a salon and had them strip the bright green color out of her hair and take out the handful of dreadlocks she'd made in the back. Colored hair isn't allowed at Awakening because they want the girls to learn who they really are inside and feel that different hair colors are a distraction to them discovering their true beauty.

The first photo Tiffany sent me was of Jennea with her natural hair color. She looked drained, like she'd been crying a lot, so it was hard to look at it. And yet it did give me a sense of peace because at least she was submitting to the process.

I kept up my main prayer and asked my family and a handful of female friends, who were all mothers, to pray that Jennea would accept the fact that she needed to stay for at least eighteen months. I knew she was miserable at first, but she needed to stay.

And I needed help.

Raising a daughter alone is hard enough, but raising a troubled teenage daughter alone is almost impossible. I obviously couldn't do it by myself any longer. I needed major female support, and I found it at Awakening Youth. Both of us did.

After the first thirty days were up, I had my very first Skype call with Jennea. Tiffany monitored the call and made it clear that Jennea was not allowed to ask me to take her out of the program. I was so nervous before the call, but after all the intense emotions and changes we had gone through, it felt so good to see my daughter again.

"Hi, Jennea," I started, my voice shaking a little. "It's so good to see you. You look great!"

"Thank you," she replied with a smile. "How are you?"

"I'm good. I've been praying for you a lot and thinking about you nonstop. Are you doing okay? Are you friends with the girls there and laughing and stuff?"

Why does this feel so awkward?

"Yes, Dad," she said with a laugh. "I laugh and I've made friends here." The video connection wasn't the greatest, but I could still see her smirking at my dumb question. And frankly, I was too happy to care how stupid I probably sounded. For weeks I had this picture in my head of Jennea all depressed and not interacting with the other girls. It was a huge relief to hear straight from her mouth that wasn't the case.

In fact, considering that the most vivid memory I had of Jennea was of her completely broken, crying, and shattered into pieces after I dropped her off, to see her smiling, laughing, and relaxed made it clear that God was already at work in her life.

One of the things that helped Jennea most was the fact that shortly after I first dropped her off at Awakening Youth, Tiffany, Travis, and all the girls moved into their new house—a beautiful eighty-five-hundred-square-foot home set atop a hill overlooking five rolling acres. The property Travis drove me to the first day I dropped Jennea off at Awakening ended up falling through, but it didn't even matter. This one was way more stunning.

Travis and Tiffany had all the girls help decorate and make the house into a home, and it was a perfect way for Jennea to bond with the other girls and become part of the group. You gotta love the timing of Jesus.

The next few Skype calls went even better than the first. We didn't get into any heavy core issues. The calls were mostly for us to focus on starting over as father and daughter, on taking baby steps toward rebuilding a civilized, healthy relationship. We were off to a great start, but the real test was our first face-to-face visit.

It was freezing cold when I arrived in Indianapolis, and thanks to the snowy roads, what should have been a forty-five-minute drive from the airport to the house took about ninety. That gave me plenty of time to think. The question that kept running through my mind was, *Is Jennea going to beg me to take her home as soon as we get alone away from Tiffany?*

There was only one way to find out.

As I came up the long driveway leading up to the house, I was in awe of the view. From the top of the hill you could see the neighbor's horses running in the snow-covered pastures below. The trees were covered in ice that sparkled like Christmas lights, and the sky was a clear, brilliant blue—the exact opposite of what it had been the day I dropped Jennea off two months earlier.

That's gotta be a good sign, right? I thought.

I was so excited about seeing Jennea that after I parked the car, I practically jogged to the front door. But before I could see Nea, Tiffany sat me down to talk about what to expect.

"She's doing really well, Brian," she said encouragingly. "We have a lot of work to do, but she's settled into the program nicely and she loves the new place."

"Okay, awesome," I said, starting to feel a little antsy. "I need to know what to do in the worst-case scenario during this visit. What if Jennea snaps like she used to and loses it on me? Or worse, what if she starts crying and begs me to take her home?"

"She's not like she was two months ago when you dropped her off," Tiffany assured me. "She's going to be fine. If something were to happen, then all you would have to do is call me and either Travis or I will be right there."

"Okay," I said, taking a deep breath. "Can I see her now?" I didn't think I could wait one minute longer.

"You sure can," she said, smiling and turning toward the stairs. "Jennea, your dad's here!"

Seconds later, Jennea appeared at the top of the stairs, and as soon as we made eye contact, she broke into the biggest smile.

"Hi, Dad!" she said.

"Hey, Nea!" I called back, feeling a slight catch in my throat.

Keep it together, Brian.

Before I knew it, Jennea was wrapped up in my arms and hugging me like crazy.

Are you kidding me? I thought. *What's going on here?* This was definitely not the cussing, cutting, depressed, lost, angry, iPhone-Twitter-Facebook-Instagram-addicted Jennea I dropped off two months ago.

"Okay, you two. Have a great visit," Tiffany said, shooing us out the door.

The cold chill of the freezing winter breeze biting at our faces, we walked to my rental car, sat down, strapped on our seat belts, and off we went.

"Where do you want to go?" I asked nervously, suddenly flashing on every detail of the heart-wrenching drop-off day just weeks prior.

"I don't know. Are you hungry?" Jennea asked.

"Yeah, are you?" I said, starting to feel slightly more at ease.

"Yeah, where do you want to eat?"

"I think I passed a Denny's on the way out here," I said. "You up for a hot breakfast?"

"Yep," she said, smiling.

Okay. Pancakes. That's a good start. Maybe this won't be as hard as I'd thought.

We passed the next few minutes making polite small talk, avoiding any mention of the program like the plague. That is, until we arrived at Denny's. Then, as I was parking the car, Jennea said eight words to me that released me from a lot of the pain that my formerly cussing, cutting, depressed, lost, angry child had put me through.

"Dad, I know I'm supposed to be here."

My heart came alive. I don't know how many times I had asked Jesus for that one major favor:

Lord, just help Jennea accept the program.

"That's awesome, Jennea," I said, trying not to make too big a deal out of it. After all, I didn't want her to think that I wanted her away from me because that wasn't the case. And just like that, instant peace was mine.

Perfection? No way. I wasn't asking for that. I just needed progress, and Jennea accepting that she was supposed to be at Awakening was a huge step in the right direction.

Wow, I thought. *What if I had just walked away when things got difficult? What if I had been so offended with God for all my trials and turned my back on him?*

I'll tell you what would've happened. I never would have been able to hear those eight golden words come out of Jennea's mouth. And I wouldn't trade those words for anything.

Over brunch at Denny's, Jennea and I talked like we hadn't talked in a long time. It was so refreshing to be in her presence. Granted, our visit wasn't perfect. In fact, I caught her sneaking online with my computer, so we had to deal with that. And she still got irritated at me, although she handled it way better than before. But compared to our full-on Christmas meltdown, those issues were practically nothing.

All in all, though, we had a great time, and it was really hard having to say good-bye again.

"I really love you, Jennea," I said when I dropped her off back at the house, "and I'm so proud of you for facing this with such maturity."

"I love you too, Dad," she said, trying not to cry as she gave me a hug.

This drop-off was hard, but it was definitely nothing like her first day—thank God.

Lord, there were so many days when the voices were screaming at me to run far away from you. They kept telling me your ways were too severe and that I wasn't ever gonna be safe with you. I was shattered in my moments of pain. But I couldn't see this wonderful day, at least not clearly. Deep down in my soul, I knew you would make something like this happen, but I couldn't see it past the pain and confusion. I could only choose to believe what I knew was buried underneath all my unbelief. And now I sit here, shining inside, feeling the touch of your tangible love and glory in my soul. I'm so glad I didn't run away from you, Jesus. I deeply and sincerely appreciate this day more than I can explain to you. I'm eternally grateful, Father. And thank you for not giving us easy fixes because we've grown so much in faith and trust in you through our pain and anguish. In Jesus' name.

I did have to tell Tiffany about the sneaking online incident because even though it was minor it was still an issue of respect—both for me as Jennea's dad and for the rules that Tiffany had put in place. Tiffany was trying to help Jennea see that she couldn't go behind my back every chance she got. That's not how you show love and respect for a person. And Jennea really did want a better relationship with me. We had struggled in a dysfunctional father-daughter relationship for too long.

Jennea had a few other hiccups during those early months at Awakening, but that was totally to be expected. And each time a negative behavior came to the surface, we dealt with it right away. And each time, Jennea rose to the occasion and learned a humongous lesson about herself. She grew and matured from every setback.

The message that Chris Overstreet gave me at Bethel Church about having a brand-new daughter in eight months was wrong. God gave me a new daughter in six months.

I was and still am so proud of Jennea. She's so beautiful inside and out, and her willingness to face the things she has faced has made me the proudest father on the planet.

———

Jennea wasn't the only person in our family who was stepping into a new season of happiness. I couldn't keep up with the amazing things happening in my life either. For example, from the day I put Jennea in Awakening Youth, I haven't experienced any rage-filled outbursts. I've been completely delivered from uncontrollable rage. On top of that, the anger I deal with now is more manageable, like what normal people deal with. I'd always wanted to experience this level of free-dom, but after praying year after year with disappointing results, it had started to seem unattainable. Until now. Finally!

So many good things were chasing me down that I couldn't keep up with them all.

At the beginning of 2013, KoRn brought in Don Gilmore, who had worked with Pearl Jam and Linkin Park, to produce our new album. By that time Jonathan had started coming around again, and everyone was pumped up and ready to start working on the new record. We had written about twenty songs, and we chose what we felt were the best fifteen to really focus on. We recorded the drum tracks at NRG Recording Studios in North Hollywood, the same studio where we'd recorded our biggest KoRn album to date, *Follow the Leader.* All of us, minus Jonathan, went to the studio to support Ray as he laid down the drum tracks. He finished in just two days.

It was really cool being back in that studio. The last time I recorded there . . . well, let's just say a lot of dark stuff was going on. Sitting around with the other guys watching Ray nail those drum tracks was another reminder of how far I'd come.

After Ray finished, it was Fieldy's turn. Recording the bass guitar is always the easiest part of doing a record, and Fieldy usually finishes all his tracks in one day—two at the most. This time around was no exception. Then it was time for Munky and me to start laying down the guitar tracks. It was on!

Maybe I'm biased, but I think guitar tracks are more fun to record than any of the other instruments. The songs completely come alive when we add the guitar parts. A lot of times Munky and I come up with new approaches as we go, and the songs end up sounding completely different than they did before.

It had been almost nine years since he and I had recorded together. We complemented each other perfectly, in my opinion. Munky is the genius, out-of-the-box creator, and I'm the grounded one who pulls together solid melody, hooks, and choruses. We're an awesome team, and the tracks came out great.

The last one into the studio was Jonathan, and he recorded all his vocals alone with Don. I got that. Ever since my epic microphone meltdowns, my respect for lead vocalists has gone through the roof. I was just grateful to be back doing what I did best—jammin' on guitar with Munky and leaving the vocals to a real vocalist.

The rest of us heard Jonathan's finished vocals one day at our producer Don's house. Despite all the severe setbacks he went through, Jonathan came out so much more positive and stronger, and he really brought his A-game on the record. I think he put down some of the best vocals he's ever done. They sounded so incredible, and he had a much wider range of melodies than what I could remember. KoRn has always been known for the raw emotion in Jonathan's lyrics and vocal delivery. Whether he sang about abuse, betrayal, hate, emptiness, being lost, or all the pain that comes with life, he has always been really open about sharing his feelings in song. Some of his lyrics do get pretty gnarly, but I love the guy and respect him. He knows where I'm at in life and where I'm coming from, and he respects me. So he deserves the same respect in return. Twenty years ago none of us cared about anyone but ourselves. Nowadays it really is the total opposite in the KoRn Kamp.

As the recording for the new album was wrapping up, we started rehearsing for our first major road tour together in over nine years. We were going to do a quick two-week run in the United States followed by a five-week tour in Europe. I couldn't wait. We rehearsed for about a week. It had been years since I'd played a lot of the songs, so I had to relearn my parts. Some of them came easy, but others, like "Falling Away from Me," were more difficult—mainly because I had to recall the guitar effect pedals that I had to press with my foot throughout. But the guys were really patient with me, and by the end of the week, we were sounding really good.

The first big show we were scheduled to play was a rock festival called Rock on the Range in Ohio that was supposed to have somewhere around a hundred thousand people in attendance.

Fortunately we also had a much smaller warm-up show a couple of days earlier in Pennsylvania, close to where Ray grew up. We met his family and friends and even got to visit his sister's zoo. She and her husband had all these exotic animals like tigers and monkeys, and we got to hold and feed a couple of them. Man, it was cool! And definitely a stress reliever.

Still, by the time the doors opened to the show, I was pretty nervous, mostly because I had to do two performances that night—one with Love and Death and one with KoRn. While I was stoked that Love and Death got to open for KoRn, I had never done two shows in one night before, and I had no idea how much that first show might take out of me. But that wasn't all. A film crew from I Am Second was also going to be there for the first few days of the tour to film for a new documentary getting released in 2016. Talk about pressure.

By the time Love and Death hit the stage, the adrenaline was flowing. We walked out on the stage, and with the cameras rolling, we went straight into our song "Paralyzed." The crowd was very receptive, and we were all stoked about how the performance went. I still loved playing with Love and Death even though I was back with KoRn, and it was great to see the crowds react so well to our music.

Luckily there was another band called Device that went on in between Love and Death and KoRn, so I was able to sneak in a little break between performances. I was glad I did because by the time KoRn hit the stage, the crowd was energized and the atmosphere was electric.

We started off with the cymbal intro to "Blind," which was our very first single almost twenty years ago. When Jonathan screamed the words, "Are you ready?!" the crowd went nuts, just like I remembered. It was as though not a single day had passed.

The next show was the big one, with somewhere around a hundred thousand screaming, metal-loving fans. The nerves I'd felt leading up to that show made the Pennsylvania show look like a cakewalk. When I walked out onto the stage to do the sound check with Love and Death that afternoon and saw how huge the stadium was, I almost lost it. We had played a ton of smaller venues and bars, and even a couple of festivals, but this was the first time Love and Death had ever opened on the main stage at a stadium, and probably the last.

When we hit the stage that afternoon, my heart felt like it

was pounding through my chest. And, of course, halfway through "Paralyzed," my mic stand broke.

Naturally.

It was a pretty good show, though, all things considered. Just like in Pennsylvania, the crowd was receptive to our music.

The funny thing is, as nervous as I was leading up to Love and Death's performance, by the time KoRn hit the stage, I was fine. Something about just playing the guitar and not having to be the front man and worry about my vocals calmed my nerves tremendously. And was that crowd into it! Hearing a thousand fans scream "Are you ready?" with Jonathan the night before was one thing, but hearing tens of thousands of people scream that night was another. The show was off the charts, and we got a massively great response from fans and critics alike. It blows my mind that my second show back with KoRn was so huge.

After the show, I got to do something that I'd never done before. I actually tattooed two of my friends, and I'm not even an artist!

A couple of friends of mine who own a tattoo shop, Ray and Kelli Putmon, had come to the show that night, and Ray had brought his tattoo equipment. I'd met Ray and Kelli a couple of years earlier while I was touring with Love and Death, and Ray had done three of my most recent tattoos. One was of a tornado going through a city on my right arm, and the others were two separate Hebrew-rooted words for God's glory, which is his glorious nature of divine love that a human being can experience. I had these two words (*Shekinah* and *Kabod*) tattooed on each of my eyelids. There's been a lot of controversy surrounding my eyelid tattoos so I'd like to explain their true meaning here:

Kabod (English transliteration; there are variations of how it is spelled) describes when a person can feel and experience God's masculine, weighty, and powerful presence or touch. *Kabod* is the masculine-rooted word for glory that is heavy and pressing, awe inspiring, and at times terrifying because it is so powerful. It is not a permanent state of being, and one doesn't always need to be a believer to experience it, as this glory does not enter inside, but rather falls on a person.

Shekinah (there are variations of how it is spelled) describes the sweet, feminine-like presence of God that a person can experience. *Shekinah* is a feminine-rooted word, meaning glory that makes a home inside, nests, dwells within. It is a very soft and subtle presence, which is why it has a feminine root. It is also a presence of shining, glowing, or radiance. It is the presence inside that slowly and gently makes our hearts God's home and begins nesting and cleaning up our lives from the inside out. This is the indwelling of the Holy Spirit and never leaves but is constant in a believer. (Certain people have a problem with God having a feminine nature in any way, but Isaiah 66:13 says God comforts us as a mother. And Genesis 1:27 says male and female were created in God's image, so God actually has both a masculine and a feminine nature.)

Anyway, after the Rock on the Range concert that night, Ray did a quick tattoo of my autograph on Fieldy's ankle to go along with all the other band members' signatures that Fieldy had gotten while I was out of the band. Fieldy almost cried because apparently ankle pain is pretty brutal. After Ray finished up with Fieldy, I picked up the gun and tattooed a cross on Ray's right arm and another one on Kelli's foot. I quickly learned that you have to be very, very steady while tattooing and make sure you put the needle in the skin just deep enough for the ink to go in. In the end, Ray's tattoo looked pretty cool—especially considering it was me who did it, but Kelli's looked like a beat-up, ugly, crooked stick figure. She was a good sport, though, and just said it looked like an old, rugged cross. Needless to say, I decided to keep my day job.

Wrapping up the two-week tour tattooing a couple of people for the first time was a great way to end my first trek with KoRn. The entire tour was great for the band—so we could get used to playing together again—and playing the bigger shows with KoRn was really beneficial for Love and Death. Tooth & Nail Records released Love and Death's first full-length album around that same time, and after the record release we had two more singles go top three at Christian Rock Radio, and our record debuted at number eighty-one on Billboard's top 200, number five on Billboard Christian Albums, number five on Billboard Hard Rock Albums, and number twenty-eight on Billboard Top Rock Albums. Not too shabby!

I slowly began to remember that though I love certain things about touring, there are other things about it that I hate. Well, maybe *hate* is a strong word. I strongly dislike some things about touring. It's not the shows I dislike; it's the traveling. We do travel in nice buses and stay in nice hotels on our days off, and for that I am truly thankful. But I can't sleep well on a tour bus, and I tend to battle with depression out on the road at times. It comes from a feeling of emptiness from not having a house to go home to every night. That's just not normal.

So even though I loved being back with my friends, the months passed by and the depression started to seep back in once in a while. I spent some nights lying awake, thinking and praying about why God led me back to KoRn.

Lord, I know you led me back to KoRn, but I really don't understand why yet. I look for opportunities to pray with people sometimes, but there aren't too many people out here who really want that. I'm sure most of these fans expect me to come back and preach at them or something. I don't want to be that guy. But I don't want to do nothing either. What should I do, Jesus? Show me what you want.

I follow you with everything in my life, and I especially need to follow you here and now.

KoRn had a couple of weeks off at the end of the summer of 2013, so one weekend I decided to visit Bethel in California again. My friends Brian and Brandon invited me to stay at one of their friend's vacant houses that weekend. We hung out, went out to eat a few times, and connected with some of the people from the band Jesus Culture, as well as members of Bethel Music. But my favorite part of that trip was the worship music. As I mentioned before, the worship that comes out of that church is nothing short of spectacular. It totally takes you away to another place.

As I was leaving one of the services, a young woman approached me.

"Hi, my name is Elizabeth. I have a word for you. Do you mind if I share it?" she asked.

"No, go for it," I confidently responded. I'd received many prophetic words in the past, so I was anxious to hear what she had to say, especially since she was a young, blonde-haired, California prophetic girl. Usually, prophetic people are weird like me, not normal like Elizabeth—hence the curiosity. Elizabeth began to speak to me about things in my life for just under ten minutes, but a name she mentioned in the first ten seconds really caught my attention.

"I feel like God is going to connect you with Todd White."

Whoa.

I had met Todd White about eight or nine years before. He had a redemption story similar to mine. One night while Todd was on a drug run gone bad, Jesus saved his life by miraculously causing a round of bullets shot directly at him to miss him and his car completely. I mean, how do you miss shooting a car by unloading a 9mm handgun from only ten feet away? The guy is a walking miracle. Anyway, right after Todd met Christ, he had this miraculous transformation, and he set out to talk to every person he came into contact with about

God's love—and I mean every person. At first he spoke with so many people about God that he started to embarrass his wife, but now she's on board, and he gets invited to speak at big events all over the world.

"Let me show you something," I said, reaching for my phone to show Elizabeth. "My friend Tommy just sent me a text a couple of weeks ago, suggesting I connect with Todd White." The young woman just looked at me and smiled. Me? I tucked the experience away to think about later.

Why does God keep bringing Todd White's name into my life?

Only a month or two later, I got a call from a filmmaker named Darren Wilson, who had released a couple of documentaries that I was a fan of.

"Hey, Brian, it's Darren Wilson from Wanderlust Productions. I got your number from Luke Billman at Shores of Grace Ministries," he said.

"Hey, Darren. Great to hear from you. I'm a big fan of your work—especially *Finger of God* and *Father of Lights*."

"Oh, wow, that means a lot. Thanks, man. Listen," he continued, "I have something crazy to ask you. I'm not sure if you'd be comfortable with this, but what would you think if I brought Todd White to a KoRn concert and filmed the two of you going out into the crowd to see what God does? I'm working on a new movie called *Holy Ghost* that the footage would be perfect for." He paused for a second. "Have you heard of Todd White?"

I couldn't help but laugh. "Well, it's funny you ask that. Not only do I know who Todd is, but in the past few months, two different people—one I've never even met before—have told me I need to connect with him. You are the third."

Now it was Darren's turn to laugh.

I thought about his idea for a minute. I felt fine about talking to groups of people in big and small churches who actually wanted to hear my story, as well as small groups of fans after shows, but taking cameras out into a metal crowd to see if God showed up? That was way outside of my comfort zone. And yet I knew how much God loves to get people out of their comfort zones and be bold, so there was only one thing to say.

"I am totally uncomfortable with going into the crowd with Todd to see if God shows up," I said. "But yes, let's do it! I actually have a tour coming up with KoRn and Rob Zombie. I'll send you the schedule to see if any of the dates make sense."

"That'd be great! Thanks, Brian."

A couple of months later, Darren and Todd caught up with us on tour, ready to start filming.

Since Fieldy was my bro in Christ, I decided to fill him in on what I was up to and see if he'd be down with getting involved. Amazingly, he wanted to be involved in every way. It turns out a friend of his had recently e-mailed him some YouTube links of Todd doing the very thing we were about to do, and Fieldy loved it. What were the odds?

Fieldy and I had done a lot of crazy stuff over the years, but we'd never done anything like this. We didn't know if the crowd would start throwing stuff at us or what. We had spent years being looked at as the cool guys, and now we were getting ready to head out into an arena full of fans to do something most of them would consider extremely uncool.

Before the show began, Todd, Darren, and the film crew approached our bus. From my window I saw Todd ask our security guard, Sleepy, if he had any pain in his leg. Sleepy said yes, and, true to form, Todd started praying for his leg. Afterward, he gave him a big hug and then came on the bus.

Man, praying for a dude like Sleepy? Now that's bold, I thought.

"Hey, Todd, what's going on, bro?" I said, hugging him.

"Hey, man! It's so good to see you," Todd said. "Listen. I love you, man, and I just want you to know, I don't want anything from you guys. I just love you. No strings at all, bro."

I need some of Todd's courage and confidence tonight, I thought.

About an hour later, after Todd had prayed with, professed his love for, and hugged my entire band, most of our crew members, and many complete strangers, we started wandering through the maze of backstage hallways, trying to figure out how to get to the fans.

"Holy Spirit, lead us to the front of the line!" I joked, trying to break the tension.

"Man, I feel like I'm gonna throw up," Fieldy mumbled nervously.

This was gonna be interesting.

The next thing we knew, we turned the corner and guess where we were? Right at the front of the line where thousands of people were walking in. *Yep.*

When the fans saw us, they screamed and applauded. Fieldy and I tried to play it cool, but inside we were both nervous wrecks. Then Todd shouted to the crowd, "Does anyone need healing in their bodies? Regardless of what you believe, we just want to pray for you."

Fieldy and I didn't know what to expect after that, but believe it or not, people responded immediately, and within fifteen minutes we had about thirty people gathered in a big huddle, praying with us for the Lord to come into their lives.

One of the people we prayed for was a mocking, half-buzzed atheist guy named Brokeback Joe, who had been suffering from back pain for years. As soon as Todd, Fieldy, and I started praying for him, right on camera, his leg grew out at least an inch. Seriously. The guy's leg actually grew right in front of our eyes. (If you don't believe me, watch the movie. It's called *Holy Ghost*, and it's incredible.) He went from mocking us to hugging us. Right then and there, I changed his name to Broke-fixed Joe. Fieldy and I were floored. I had seen stuff like that happen right before my eyes before, so it wasn't a total shock for me, but it was so cool to get it captured on video for the movie.

All right, Lord, you showed up once. Don't let that be the last time tonight.

And it wasn't.

After the show, we went back out and prayed with people again. A few of Rob Zombie's crew were a little annoyed because our praying was taking sales away from the merch tables, but we didn't let that stop us. We moved to a different spot and kept praying. There were many fans in tears, telling us how broken they were. It was crazy how receptive they were. We met people that night who were dealing with alcohol abuse, family problems, health issues—you name it—and the love of Jesus was touching them all. Many of them invited the Lord into their lives that night, and it changed mine and Fieldy's lives. It was so amazing to see the Lord show up and display the power of his love in an aggressive place like a metal concert.

Since that day we have prayed with at least two thousand fans after our concerts. Nowadays, we even bring a guy with us on the road whose main duty is to go out into the crowd, asking God to lead him to fans who may be open to receiving Jesus. He then invites thirty to one hundred fans to meet Fieldy and me, and we spend an hour or so telling them our stories and about the love and forgiveness of Jesus for each and every one of them. We see God show up all the time, and the stories we hear are incredible.

There was one girl who had done bath salts and was run over by a diesel truck and had her legs crushed. She'd been in a wheelchair for months. After hearing us speak by accidentally stumbling upon us talking to fans on her way out of a concert one night, she started letting God into her life more and more, and he is continuing to show her signs of his presence in her life. I just got word recently that she got out of her wheelchair and walked again for the first time since the accident.

Then there was the sixteen-year-old girl who privately confessed to me and Fieldy that she was trying to kill her friend by poisoning her. She asked for forgiveness and then asked Jesus into her life while we prayed for her.

Another guy was drunk in line, waiting to get a photo with us, and he was so blitzed that he staggered up to us and slurred out, "Where's the after-party?" and then collapsed on us as we pushed him back up. After we finished meeting all the fans in line, the dude got it together a little. He confessed he had recently gotten his third DUI and wouldn't have a license for another fifteen years. He was only twenty-three. Fieldy and I prayed for him, asked Christ to intervene in his life, and less than an hour later, he walked away sober and looking like a completely different person.

I could go on and on, but you get the idea. People are hurting, and Jesus wants to reach out to them. Unfortunately, a lot of people either hate or distrust religion, and as a result won't set foot in a church. So what does Jesus do? He sends out people like us to reach them. And do you know what? Jesus isn't afraid of some foul lyrics in a metal song. He cares about these people's lives, and he wants their hearts.

And for the most part people around us are receptive, but we do sometimes get ridiculed by friends and fans. Some guys in our camp call mine and Fieldy's bus the Holy Roller bus behind our backs, but we're not uptight, so we don't mind. We can dish it right back to those fools. One night when we were sharing our testimonies, people started walking by, laughing and yelling "666! Hail Satan!" So we just spoke louder.

"Laugh at us all you want, but how many of you have lost someone because of drugs?" I asked. About fifty people raised their hands. "I'd be dead right now because of my addictions if it weren't for Jesus coming into my life and saving me," I continued. "We are out here because we love you guys. Jesus, who is God, came into our lives and changed us, and he will come make his home inside of you and change you from the inside out. Jesus said, 'Come to me.' He doesn't care what you are or what you've done. He loves you right where you're at. He only wants you to come to him!"

"If that's you," Fieldy continued, "if you need a fresh start, if you need Jesus in your life, just raise your hand, and we'll all pray together."

Nowadays, we reach out to fans like this whenever God leads. Sometimes it's entire tours, and sometimes it's only a few shows during a tour. We want to be led. We don't want to force things on people prematurely. The fans' hearts have to be ready to receive, and only the Spirit can prepare hearts.

People have asked me, "What's your favorite part about your ministry to your fans?"

My favorite part is that Jesus shows up and shows off. So why not go back to KoRn and hang out with these people? Didn't Jesus leave all his perfection and beauty from his spiritual paradise at home as a King on his throne to come to the earth to hang out with us dirty, lying, cheating, messed-up, selfish humans? Are any of us better than the fans at KoRn concerts? *No!* Every single human being on the planet is just as in need of God's love as the next.

We all need Jesus, and my mind has been thoroughly blown away by the fact that I was chosen for this extremely unique call into the metal scene.

As the time passed by with me being reunited with KoRn and Jennea anchored in Awakening Youth, I couldn't keep up with all the amazing things happening to us. The effects of the transformation taking place in Jennea kept increasing. It was staggering that after falling into a black hole of nothingness months earlier, she was now blossoming like a rose at Awakening Youth. Every time I saw or talked to her, she seemed healthier and happier than the time before. I can't tell you how grateful I am to God and Awakening Youth for everything he has done and is continuing to do for her.

At the time of this writing, she is still at Awakening Youth. The original program was supposed to go for eighteen months, but things were going so incredibly well that we all decided (including Jennea) she should stay there—at least until she graduates from high school, and possibly even longer.

About a year ago I got a condo near the school so I could live close to her and see her as much as possible. Watching her grow from an insecure, depressed, lonely teenager into a strong, confident, and beautiful young woman has been one of the greatest blessings of my life.

I waited until I was an adult to face all the ugly truths about myself. But Jennea? She tackled her demons before she even started driving. She truly is my hero, and I genuinely look up to her. She's going to change so many people's lives. I can't wait to see the journey that Jesus takes her on.

I also can't wait to see the journey that Jesus takes me on in the years ahead. The past ten years haven't always been easy, in fact some of it has been totally excruciating, as you have just read. But through it all, Jesus has remained faithful. In spite of all my attacks, trials, persecutions, failings, meltdowns, and mistakes, he has never once abandoned me. And he never will.

Recently I got to attend an end-of-the-year family formal at Awakening Youth. Jennea dressed up like a princess, and I even wore a tuxedo. It was so beautiful to see everyone honor the girls for their hard work. They all looked stunningly beautiful, and the waiters and waitresses did a dance in unison as they served our plates of food. There was even a dance party after our first-class dinner was over. The dance party was mainly for the girls to let loose and party, but halfway through they played a song for a father-daughter dance. Talk about emotional. I had a glimpse of what it's gonna be like at Jennea's wedding. Scary and exciting!

Holding Jennea in my arms and dancing with her was such a dichotomy of what our lives were like only two years before. God is so good and so kind that he just leaves me speechless.

Right now Jennea and I are both living out what Romans 8:28 really means: "And we know that God causes everything to work together for the good of those who love God and are called according to his purpose for them" (NLT).

It's been a wild ride. And personally, I can't wait to see what happens next.

EPILOGUE

As I head into 2016, almost a full decade after having walked away from KoRn, it's hard to believe how much my life has changed. Sometimes when I stop to think about everything I've been through—the depression, the lawsuits, the betrayals, the bankruptcy, and all the challenges Jennea and I faced together—I feel like I've been put to death and raised back to life again and again.

As difficult and as painful as my experiences were, they needed to happen. Yeah, I got knocked down a lot, but each time I got back up, I got back up stronger.

And wiser.

When I first encountered Christ, I thought I had to prove to God how much faith and trust I had in him. I thought that *was* faith. But now I know that faith isn't something you prove; it's something you possess. It's not external. It's internal. And it isn't about taking control and doing things your way. It's about abandoning control and letting God do his work through you.

I sometimes selfishly wish that I could finally leave this planet to be with the divine unseen One whom I have come to love, and whom I've learned is more real than anyone or anything I can see with my natural eyes. But being a true Christ-follower is saying, "Jesus, I give myself to you completely. Do whatever you want with me and with my life. Give me the desires of your heart so I can pray in agreement with what you want to do with me. I am only clay. Mold me into a beautiful work of art."

And that is exactly what he has done.

I just didn't always see it.

I used to think God wanted me to walk away from KoRn and the metal scene forever. But now I know that God's real purpose in leading me away from that world was not to remove me from it completely; it was to prepare me to go back into it. I needed to get stronger physically, emotionally, and spiritually so I could go back and be a light in the darkness for millions of lost and hurting people—people who may never set foot in a church, but who will come out to hear us play and lose themselves in our music.

Over the past ten years, Jesus has walked with me through the most intense suffering of my life—not to punish me, but to cleanse me. Everything I went through—the nightmares with Edgar, the labels backing out, the lawsuits, the repossessions, losing the house, and being sued by friends (most of which I caused through my own careless financial decisions)—was God's way of bringing all the worst traits in me to the surface so he could take them away from me once and for all.

It's like I was a wild horse that Jesus had to break. When everything was being taken away from me—my house, my cars, my money, and even my friends—it revealed my lack of trust and satisfaction in God alone, which is what he wanted from me all along, mainly because that was also what I had asked Jesus for in my own life.

The Bible says that our heavenly Father disciplines us in order to correct what is wrong in us (Hebrews 12:6)—in other words, to bring about healing. And let me tell you, God has been healing me through discipline and suffering for years. That's why one of the many nicknames for God is the Great Physician. Just like a surgeon has to cut a patient open in order to correct what's wrong, God has to cut into our souls in order to correct what's wrong in us. He cuts and he cuts until all we bleed is the character and nature of his beloved Son, Jesus. And man, does the cutting hurt.

But all the hurt we endure ends up being totally worth it because a profound, mystical, and miraculous exchange can be experienced through suffering. Through the refining fire of adversities, God takes out pieces of our humanity and replaces it with his divine nature. As astounding as it sounds, we are slowly being changed into the mirror image of Jesus from the inside out. None of us can try and be good enough to act like Jesus in our own strength. God has to supernaturally form Jesus in us as we submit to the sometimes difficult and other times fun process (Galatians 4:19; Romans 8:29).

When I think about Jesus shining brighter than the sun and appearing in different forms as it says in the Bible, I get very excited. We will have a measure of this one day as well. But we have to remember that God is humility itself. Jesus is the very definition of love and servanthood, which is the exact nature God is forming in us as he slowly transforms us through our sufferings. Revelations like this help make suffering so much easier to endure.

Many times over the past ten years I've felt like I could identify with the long-suffering biblical character Job. If you're not familiar with Job, he faced three different trials: he lost all his possessions, his family, and his health. But his life ended up better than it was before his suffering. In fact, God gave him everything back and more. I also lost most of my possessions. I lost Jennea for a while to self-harm and suicidal issues. I also went through some health issues I wouldn't wish on anyone and suffered emotional anguish so intense it was almost crippling.

Did I complain a lot? Oh yeah. But I never quit. And today I am stronger than I've ever been. Things that used to send me over the edge can't even touch me now. I have an ocean of peace living inside me that nothing can disturb. And that very ocean of peace is the feeling of the intense glory of heaven in my mind, will, and emotions as the transfiguration does its work year after year to reveal Christ's splendor inside of me. I am telling you by experience, having Christ's beautiful, supernatural, divine soul formed inside of my natural human soul makes every bit of suffering worth it. If I had to, I would go through all the suffering again in order to feel this miraculous change, because in some ways my mind and emotions feel more angelic than human a lot of the time now. I'm not trying to sound weird or too deep; I'm only sharing what I have personally experienced. This is what Jesus died to create—a new humanity. A new species. We shouldn't be limited by only feeling human inside anymore.

For those of you who still struggle with your life, I can promise you, as you choose to give control over to Christ, you'll see him show up in incredible ways—just when you need it most. Seriously. Every time. I am still far from perfect, and I still have to choose to give control over to Jesus again and again because my flesh is weak, man. So weak. Just recently I fell into something that I want to share with you because I've always been real with you. To make a long story short, I started drinking wine with communion, and it seemed harmless enough. But then after going through some relationship difficulties, I ended up drinking alone at home, doing fireball shots of whiskey at bars, and sometimes drinking a twelve pack of beer a night. I turned into an alcoholic again off and on for a couple of months, but do you know what I didn't do? I didn't quit. I talked to Jesus while I was drunk, I talked to Jesus after I threw up, I talked to Jesus all the time, and now I'm doing better than I was doing before that fall.

God has loved me to freedom—freedom from addiction, from rage, from greed, from rejection, from bitterness and mistrust—and he'll do it for every single person reading this book as long as you keep your relationship with him going and never, ever quit.

And now I'm playing shows around the world with my childhood friends, watching Jesus do things through Fieldy and me that I could never have imagined in my wildest dreams. I grew up with my KoRn brothers, and I'm having so much fun traveling the world and playing these crazy songs with them. I may not always agree with what Jonathan's lyrics say, but I agreed with his lyrics at one point, so I can relate to all the fans that still love them today. Those songs are a part of my history. They're part of my story.

So is God.

First Corinthians 9:22 says, "I have become all things to all people . . ."

So for now I'm just gonna do what I've been called to do: play my music, show unfailing love to my daughter and to all our fans, and, most important, continue to love God above all else and to engage as much as possible with the spiritual world that Jesus died to give me.

I want it all, and I'm just getting started. I haven't even scratched the surface yet.

Come and join me.

And remember, "Above all, have fervent and unfailing love for one another, because love covers a multitude of sins" (1 Peter 4:8 AMP).

A NOTE FROM JENNEA

Dear Reader,

I'm writing you from my bedroom window as I watch the August wind move the trees. What a picturesque view—I wish everyone was able to experience this.

I used to not see the world as I do now. In my past, the trees seemed dull, the wind cold, and I couldn't understand the reason behind life; nor did I want to. I felt inadequate and always saw myself lower than everyone I came in contact with. I found myself in such a dark place, constantly seeking attention and love when I was looking in all the wrong places. I had let self-harm, depression, angst, hate, loneliness, and suicidal thoughts govern over me. What a horrible thing, to believe that you are worthless compared to the world around you.

As I contemplate my past and all the thoughts that come with it, I find myself gazing at the trees. Each one of them is built uniquely, beautifully, thoughtfully, and intricately. How could someone not believe that they are so much more valuable than the trees that surround them?

This book is in your hands for a specific reason. I hope that it will be a reminder of your worth. You do not need to compare yourself or change who you are to feel whole. You do not need to harm yourself or degrade yourself in any way to relieve what's going on inside of your head—and your heart. So many people have believed that these are the paths to comfort, and what a lie that is! Despite what you've been through and what you're going through now, your value is evident. You were chosen, planned, and formed by a God who longs for you and wants you to see the masterpiece that he designed you to be.

I'm so glad you are able to look inside the story of my family. Looking from the outside, it's easy to believe that we have it all together; but the truth is that we are as broken as the next person. It was just a matter of letting God mend together the missing holes that separated us. The goal for my dad and me through this book was to show people that they are not alone in their sufferings, and that they should hold fast and know that it can change for the good. You are so incredibly loved and wanted, and I hope our story can bring you hope, joy, peace, under-standing, and revelation. Be inspired, and know that you are not alone in this.

Jennea

A NOTE FROM BRIAN

I want you to take a minute and think back on the last five years of your life.

Did they go by fast?

Yeah, mine too.

There are over seven billion people living on the earth right now—and counting. We all need to come to the realization that in only a few decades, all those people will be gone, and the earth will be filled with all new people.

We're all passing through like the earth is a McDonald's drive-through window, and most of us usually end up ordering the most unhealthy things for our lives. The fast track we're on is only meant to prepare us to get back to where we were all meant to be—resting in God's heart.

Like a bride in her husband's arms, we are all meant to find our true rest in Jesus because he is the only lover of our souls able to fulfill our deepest, most hidden desires. But that inner rest doesn't start the day we die and leave this planet.

It all starts the day we step into Christ and enter into God's rest through faith. It can start *now*. And this direction in Colossians is a great example of how we stay in rest:

> Set your minds and keep focused habitually on the things above [the heavenly things], not on things that are on the earth [which have only temporal value]. For you died [to this world], and your [new, real] life is hidden with Christ in God. (Colossians 3:2–3 AMP)

It's a heavenly reality, my friends. Yes, it may seem mystical, but it is also real and tangible.

Jesus is not some handsome white dude from history with long hair, a robe, and sandals like in the movies. He is God's only answer for this hurting world, and the only one who will lead us into God's true rest.

When I say rest, I don't mean sleep. I'm describing a position in God's heart, in the spiritual dimension, that is handed to you now and will be your place in God forever. It's a place of peace and indescribable happiness that surpasses all understanding. A high nobody has ever achieved on this planet—one that comes from the highest source of glory available. A love that never fades. A person—the only person—who never *has* and never *will* let any of us down in the end.

Look: I know pain. And I know you do too. God cares deeply about all our pain. You just read my story—I had close to a decade of what most would call bad luck. I could've given God the finger and walked away.

But I didn't.

You know why?

Because I knew he would come through and bring indescribable happiness out of my pain. Whether it took him one year, two, or many years down the line, I knew he would come through for me and Jennea in some way, turn around every injustice we were battling, and bring lasting happiness from it.

I was right.

You just read it, and I just lived it.

And I'm still living it.

I said this before, but I need to say it again because it's true.

I.

Am.

Barely.

Getting.

Started.

I hope you took notice of my amazingly happy, changed life. Because God can—and will—do the same for you.

I'm hoping there will be a lot of good things to come from this book, but nothing would make me happier than for as many of you as possible to pray these words with me and *mean them from your heart.*

Jesus,

Right now, take my life into your hands completely. As I enter into a nonstop search for you, please make everything brand-new inside me, and let me feel the effects of my new life starting right now. Forgive me, wash away all the residue of my past from this day backward, make everything brand-new, and turn all of the dirtiness from my past into something beautiful from this day forward. Lord, open my spiritual eyes and ears so that I can see and understand that the spiritual world is very real. Help me believe that it's more real than anything I can see with my eyes on earth because one day these earthly eyes will stop seeing completely. Reveal your love to me and show me how to truly love you back.

Amen.

ACKNOWLEDGMENTS

I want to give a sincere and heartfelt thank you to you, Jennea, for being so secure in yourself that you let me share your darkest struggles with the world. I love you.

To all my family, friends, and fans—I wouldn't be here without all of you. Thank you so much.

Thank you to Bryan Norman and David Williams for seeing the initial idea for this book when I couldn't.

Everyone at Thomas Nelson—thank you for believing in this project and for all your hard work:

Brian Hampton, *publisher*

Jessica Wong, *senior acquisitions editor*

Janene MacIvor, *senior editor*

Katherine Rowley, *editor*

DJ Lipscomb, *marketing manager*

Kristen Gathany, *art director*

Carol Traver, thank you so much. This book would not be what it is without your help.

Jasen Rauch, I told you I am your biggest fan, and I mean it! Thank you for inspiring me to pick up my guitar and play like *ME* again. Your inspiration helped prepare me to jump back on the KoRn train.

Thank you to Nick Raskulinecz—there's no reason to put your name in this book, but you kept asking me to, so here you go, haha!

Kelli Putmon, thank you for the wisdom from your Hebrew word study. Keep going after the mysteries, girl.

Ray Putmon, thank you for not letting the tattoo needle poke through my eyelid into my eyeball.

I want to honor the late Father Thomas Edward Dubay, S.M., for writing the book *The Fire Within*. Though I am not a Catholic, the truths he wrote about the soul and its ability to fly, if you will, into a deep immersion in God, even while living on earth in our bodies, has changed my life by experiencing those very things many times over. If you desire to experience Jesus in a deep, close, personal, intimate, and supernatural way, and you don't want to feel like he's galaxies away from you, this book is the best road map I've found. I will read it over and over the rest of my life. (Disclaimer: I don't agree with every single detail in the book. But most of it. I decided long ago to just "eat the meat and spit out the bones," like I do with every other book I read and speaker I hear. Nobody is perfect except you know Who.)

God . . . my love, my life—my everything. I am so grateful beyond words for this book and everything else you do *for* me, as well as *through* me, to touch others.

ABOUT THE AUTHOR

Brian "Head" Welch was born June 19, 1970, and grew up in Bakersfield, California. He found his calling at age eleven when he picked up his first guitar. Voracious practicing and a steady diet of hard rock classics filled the ensuing years, and shortly after high school he cofounded the rock band named KoRn. The band soon became a Grammy Award–winning, multi-platinum force that shot to the top tier of the rock world and dominated the nu metal movement from the late nineties and beyond. Brian received six Grammy nominations, winning two, while selling some 40 million records worldwide.

As KoRn continued to reach new creative and commercial heights, Brian found himself drowning in the excesses of rock and roll. Far from immune to the slings and arrows of outrageous fortune, Brian became addicted to crystal meth, spiraling out of control even as he continued to sell millions of albums. He gamely but unsuccessfully tried to balance his career and his obligations as a single father to his daughter, Jennea. In 2005, Brian finally resigned from KoRn and turned to Christ, dedicating his life to learning how to get to know his very personable God and giving his gifts to those most desperately in need.

Having experienced such grievous personal lows amid the professional highs, Brian felt compelled to recount his life before and after KoRn. His autobiography, *Save Me from Myself* (HarperCollins), released in 2007 and became a *New York Times* bestseller. Feeling inspired, Brian also wrote a very personal forty-day devotional, *Stronger*, sharing stories about the forty scriptures closest to his heart.

Brian continues his charitable efforts both in the United States and across the globe—giving whatever he can to the neediest—and strives to be the best possible father to his beloved daughter, Jennea.

If you or someone you know needs help with a teen or young adult, please contact (765) 296-5418 or visit www.awakeningyouth.net.

Get Love and Death's new single "Lo Lamento"
<u>FREE</u> with the purchase of the book *With My Eyes Wide Open*

http://www.brianheadwelch.net/freesingle

Also available:

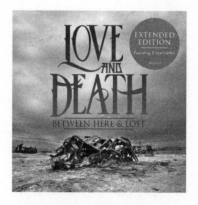

Save Me From Myself   Between Here & Lost

Visit http://store.brianheadwelch.net,
the official store for all things Brian Head Welch

a
FEATURE DOCUMENTARY
COMING SOON

facebook.com/brianheadwelch
brianheadwelch.net

I AM SECOND®

real stories. changing lives. **iamsecond**.com

BRIAN "HEAD" WELCH
Lead Guitarist for the band Korn

ANNIE LOBERT
Founder of Hookers for Jesus

RYAN RIES
Co-Founder of The Whosoevers